STORIES OF OLD GIPPSLAND

Other books by Jim Connelly

Tom and Anna on the Trail (2014)

Tom and Anna in Danger (2014)

Tom and Anna take a Chance (2015)

My Folk: 400 Years of Hazards, Tooths, and Connellys (2015)

Mountain Boy (2016)

Talk of the Town: Warragul/Drouin (2017)

Talk of the Town (2): Warragul/Drouin (2018)

Pickled Pieces and Rollicking Rhymes (2019)

Wild Beauty (2019)

Round and About in Gippsland (2020)

Father Jeremy (2020)

Growing up in Garfield (2021)

STORIES OF OLD GIPPSLAND

Jim Connelly

Copyright

A CIP catalogue record for this book is available from the

National Library of Australia.

First published in Australia 2022 by

James Timothy Connelly

12 Craig Street

Warragul, Victoria, 3820

AUSTRALIA

ajcon@dcsi.net.au

For Elizabeth, Catherine, Christopher, and Richard

Cover design by Craig Braithwaite, *aussiepics*

CONTENTS

Stories of old Gippsland

FOREWORD

Gippsland's past abounds with strange and extraordinary stories. It is important that we keep alive these foundational tales of ours. Although these stories are well known to a smallish circle of interested people, I find that the majority of Gippslanders are quite unaware of these tales from their past. The object of this book is to bring to a wider audience a handful of these old stories so that our past may be more generally treasured.

I make no claim to originality in presenting these old tales of Gippsland. Splendid work is being done throughout the region in Historical Societies and by individuals. People like Patrick Morgan and Linda Barraclough – and many others like them – have done amazing work in opening up our history and putting it into a historical and philosophical context. I am standing on the shoulders of many more learned folk than I in daring to offer these tales to the public. My hope is that through their relatively short form and more personalised style they may attract interest and so encourage others to delve into our history and extend our understanding of the past.

Jim Connelly
May, 2022

Lennie Rides Alone

I've been looking through the records of long-distance horse-rides. I've read of some amazing rides. Belinda Fane rode from Gosford to Perth in 1963, although she put her horses on the train across the Nullarbor. Nothing I read, however, was a patch on the celebrated solo ride of Lennie Gwyther from Leongatha to Sydney – and return. And Lennie was nine years old, ten when he got back!

Lennie's ride has been written up many times. Books and songs have been written about it, radio programs and videos made. Yet I meet people all the time who have never heard of this young Gippsland hero. One man had lived in Leongatha for forty years, yet knew nothing of the ride. It's for him and people like him that I re-tell the story. To give my account some freshness, I'll try to use the newspaper accounts of the time as far as I can.

First, it's important to know the stock that Lennie came from. It helps to understand the grit he showed in his great endeavour. His grandfather Gwyther was one of the pioneers of the Leongatha district, going back to 1875. Lennie's mother was a Simon, also from an early settler family. Lennie's father, was one of five boys. They all enlisted in the First World War. Lennie's father, Leo Tennyson Gwyther, joined up two weeks after war was declared. He had a stellar war record, serving at Gallipoli, and in France and Belgium. He rose through the ranks to become Captain Leo Gwyther. He was wounded twice, and gassed. He won the Military Cross *and* Bar for 'conspicuous gallantry in action'. He returned to farm just south of Leongatha on a property he called 'Flers' after the place in France where he had won the first of his Military Crosses.

Lennie combined his schooling with working on the farm. In fact, that's how the ride came about. In 1932, Lennie's father broke his leg and was unable to carry out the farm work. This was left to the boy. He explained to a reporter in Sydney:

Last Melbourne Show holidays, when my father was in hospital, I harrowed and smoged* with a four-horse team twenty-four acres of land. And on account of my doing so, my Dad was so pleased that he said I could go on my present trip to Sydney to see the opening of the Harbour Bridge. (*Smoge: to smooth, probably with the harrows turned upside down.)

Both mother and father were apprehensive about the scheme, but eventually agreed, though not without making arrangements for some of Lennie's travelling arrangements along the way. Lennie, along with the rest of Australia, had been fascinated by newspaper reports of the building of the Harbour Bridge. The Bridge was set to be opened on the nineteenth of March, 1932. Lennie left on the third of February. The distance, through Cooma, was 925 kilometres or 575 miles, as they reckoned it in those days. He carried a water-bottle and a pack with spare clothes, a toothbrush, and pyjamas – and £1 in his pocket. He habitually wore a rain hat covering the back of his neck. We used to call them 'sou-westers'. His horse, 'Ginger Mick', was also nine years old, the same as Lennie himself.

There were difficulties. He hadn't gone far before a 'mad swagman' caused him some trouble. Through Traralgon he rode through the dense smoke of nearby bushfires. Lennie rode on. He was now expected as he reached each town. People came out to meet him. They provided him with meals. He slept in private homes and hotels by prior arrangement or by warm invitation. There is no record of whether he ever sent messages home, but his progress was well-known to his family through the newspaper reports of

11

his journey. He rode through Mirboo North and Morwell, then along the highway to Cann River. From here he turned north along the Cann Valley to Bombala and Cooma. In Canberra, then just a small country town, he had afternoon tea with the Prime Minister, Joseph Lyons, and played games with the boys at Canberra Grammar School. Then on to Sydney. He arrived in Martin Place on the fifth of March with a mounted police escort amidst an estimated 10,000 onlookers.

Lennie's father had travelled by train to Sydney and was there to facilitate Lennie's arrangements. The 'Sun' newspaper took Lennie in hand. He took in the sights - Circular Quay, Bondi Beach, and Taronga Park Zoo. He was given an inspection tour of the Bridge itself. I can't find any reference to where Ginger Mick was all this time. However, on the great day of the Opening, Lennie and Ginger Mick took their places in the Grand Parade ready to cross the bridge. There are photos of horse and rider waiting patiently for the Parade to begin, Lennie wearing his sou-wester as always. Up ahead, another rider on another horse tried to spoil the proceedings. Major Francis de Groot belonged to a right-wing, neo-Fascist group called the 'New Guard'. Just before the Premier, Jack Lang, could cut the ribbon to mark the official opening, de Groot rode out of the crowd and slashed the ribbon, shouting, 'In the name of the decent and loyal citizens of New South Wales I declare this Bridge open!' He was hustled away, the ribbon was restored, and the formalities resumed. Ginger Mick carried his rider safely past the official dais, across the bridge – and back again.

Lennie and his father stayed in Sydney a little longer. They went to the Easter Show, where Lennie and Ginger Mick competed in one event. They went to the Sydney Cricket Ground, where Don Bradman gave Lennie an autographed cricket bat. The plan was that Lennie, his father, and Ginger Mick would take a steamer back to Melbourne. However, Lennie had come to enjoy being the centre of attraction. He pleaded with his father that he be allowed to ride his horse home again, and his father, whom I suspect was rather enjoying being the Father of the Boy, agreed. A triumphal return procession began, this time through inland New South Wales. At Gunning, he spoke to the schoolchildren and attended a meeting of the Shire Council where he was presented with a £1 note for his tenth birthday. He spent two nights as the guest of the local squatting family, the Falkiners, at Widgiewa. At Urana he was given a reception and attended the annual Children's Ball. "His pony has a set trot," the local paper reported. "He seldom canters his mount, and gets along at an even five miles per hour". The Lockhart Review's report may be taken as typical of his reception along the route of his 'royal tour'

On arriving at the Reserve Lennie was surrounded by the Lockhart Boy Scouts. ... The Scouts, with national colours flying, escorted him along the main street to the School of Arts where the girls of the Junior Red Cross Circle ... welcomed him with cheers led by the Shire President. ... His pony was taken charge of by Mr W G Campbell, blacksmith, Lockhart. ... When the time came for him to leave Lockhart he had a well-fed, well-groomed pony to start the journey with. Entering the hall, Lennie made his way through the crush of people on to the stage. ... Mrs Meldrum, Cr Nolan, Mr Scott and Rev Graham made speeches of welcome and applauded his plucky performance.... Closer acquaintance with Lennie confirmed ... that he was a boy amongst boys, glowing with health, subdued but not lacking in spirit and of modest mien. ... Lennie's modest reply to all the kind things said about him was 'Thank you very much'.

And so on to Albury and 'down the Hume Highway' to Melbourne, where more adulation and another civic reception awaited him. Lennie reached home on the twelfth of June, 133 days after he had set out, and went back to school.

Lennie later married. He served in the RAAF during the Second World War, and then worked as an engineer at General Motors Holden at Fisherman's Bend. He made his home in Hampton, and died at the age of seventy in 1992. He seldom referred to his boyhood achievement. In 2017 a statue of Lennie and Ginger Mick was erected in Leongatha. Lennie's sister, aged 92, his daughter, and sixty members of the wider Gwyther family were present.

More than a Bullock Driver

The story of Agnes Buntine is widely known, but as the memories of Agnes and her bullock wagon fade further and further into the past, so it becomes more and more necessary to re-write her story for modern ears. For one thing, we might ask how this unlearned woman of the bush came to be within a couple of generations the matriarch of a family that included some of the intellectual and business leaders of society. It's a great tale of social mobility and suggests that Australia truly has been a 'land of opportunity'.

I think Agnes was as much Scottish doggedness as she was Australian adventurism. She came with her family, the Davidsons, from their small farm at Mauchline, south of Glasgow, to Melbourne in 1840, when Melbourne was little more than a clutch of shanties. The next year they moved on to Port Albert, where Agnes married Hugh Buntine, a recent widower and close friend of the family. The Buntines were former neighbours in Scotland and had persuaded the Davidsons to emigrate. The next year, 1841, a son was born at Port Albert. He was named Albert and was the first white child born in Gippsland. It is through this that Agnes is often referred to as 'Mother Buntine' – 'Mother of Gippsland'.

Hugh and Agnes were true Gippsland pioneers. They moved on to a small place near Tarraville where they ran cattle and kept a bush inn. But they had grander plans. In 1845, they took up the original lease of Bruthen Creek station, 8,000 acres of undeveloped country. Bruthen Creek is nowhere near the town of Bruthen. It runs from the Strzeleckis, passes close to Woodside, and reaches the coast near McLaughlin's Beach. Life was still precarious. Hugh opened an inn in a slab hut on the Sale Road, while it was from here that Agnes began her legendary career as a bullock driver.

It began in 1851, very shortly after the start of the gold rushes. Agnes loaded a wagon with cheese and salted butter, a ton and a half in weight, hitched up her team and set off for the McIvor diggings near Bendigo. Bullock teams typically travel at about three miles an hour. That's when the going is good and the road is constructed. Agnes had some 230 miles to travel along a route she had never seen, alone and unattended, seeing to the feeding and watering of the animals, sleeping at night under the wagon, at a time when colonial society was unsettled and largely unpoliced. At the diggings she set up a store where she sold her butter and cheese as well as general goods. Within a short time she had established at least one other store. It was two years before she returned to Bruthen Creek. To add to her curriculum vitae, Agnes had five children at this time and a sixth was soon to be born.

Hugh and Agnes gave up Bruthen Creek within a few years. Hugh was not well and Agnes was carrying more and more of the family burden. In 1858 the family moved to Flynn's Creek, east of Rosedale. Agnes used this as her base as she set up a more regular carrying service between Melbourne and the rapidly-extending settlements throughout Gippsland. One story has it that she was trapped in a bush fire on one occasion and barely escaped with her life.

When the Walhalla rush began in 1862, Agnes began a more or less regular carrying service between Port Albert and Walhalla, bringing in provisions and machinery. Heavy machinery for the diggings would be unloaded at the port and Agnes would carry it to Walhalla, some eighty miles away. The Gippsland Times ran a story on Agnes back in 1932, where it was claimed that Agnes was running two bullock teams at this stage. The man in charge of the other team was accidentally wounded by a gun shot. Agnes patched him up, put him on a horse and sent him off to the nearest doctor, while she took over both teams for the rest of the journey. I think she must have had some good dogs to help her.

And what of Agnes herself? One photo of her has survived, taken later in her life. It shows a heavy–featured woman, almost masculine, with a look in her eye that says, 'Don't mess with me!' She habitually wore leggings, heavy boots, and a thick shawl. She smoked a pipe, carried a gun, and mostly had a whip in her hand, which she used to good effect if she came across a scene of injustice or cruelty. Tom McDonald was a fellow-bullocky who knew her well:

I used to meet Agnes Buntine often, yarn with her, and share each other's tobacco. She smoked an old black pipe – and plug tobacco at that. ... Anyhow, she did a man's work, so why shouldn't she smoke a man's pipe? ... She could drive a team of bullocks as good as any bullock driver in Gippsland. The way the bullock wagons went from Port Albert to Walhalla must have been 80 miles or more. The journey took many days, eight at least. At night Agnes Buntine used to roll herself up in a blanket and sleep under the pole of the wagon.

Agnes was more than a bullock driver. She turned her hand to all kinds of farm and rural work, from fencing to cattle mustering. She had a reputation for personal kindness, although there are stories of her rough treatment of aborigines.

After Hugh's death she married a man in his late 'twenties (she was in her fifties) and lived on at Flynn, on the farm, until her death in 1896, aged seventy-three or seventy-four. Agnes died in the Sale Hospital and was buried in the Rosedale Cemetery. Strangely, the site seems to have been unmarked. No one has ever been able to find her grave.

Agnes's family has gone on to make a considerable mark on the nation. Her son, Robert Buntine farmed at Rosedale, and his son, Agnes's grandson, Walter Murray Buntine, became a leading educationalist, a member of the Melbourne University Council and of several other statutory educational bodies. The Australian Biographical Dictionary describes him as an 'Anglican lay leader, educational reformer, school owner, school principal, and schoolteacher'. At one time he was the owner of Caulfield

Grammar School which has always had a strong connection with Gippsland.

Walter Murray Buntine's son, Agnes's great-grandson, Martyn Arnold Buntine, became the headmaster, successively, of Camberwell Grammar, Hale School, Perth, and Geelong College. He is remembered as one the most distinguished educators this State has known. (And his wife, Gladys, was Chief Commissioner of Girl Guides for Australia for many years).

The Buntine tentacles don't end there. A grandson, William Odell Raymond Buntine became one of Australia's leading actors, writers, and film directors in the early days of cinema. He took the name of Talone (Tal) Ordell. He played the part of Dave in '*On our Selection*', while his film, '*The Kid Stakes*' is regarded as a triumph of early Australian filmcraft. Noel Buntine, a great-great-grandson of Agnes, became a leading businessman, landowner, and racing identity in the Northern Territory. The Buntine Pavilion in the Road Transport Hall of Fame at Alice Springs is named for him, as is also the Buntine Highway between Willaroo and Nicholson in Western Australia.

21

I wonder if Agnes ever dreamed – as she plodded along behind her bullock team - of the part her family would play in the development and enrichment of our national community.

The Black-Allan Line

Gippsland has a long boundary with New South Wales and it's not to be taken for granted. The next time you speed through the border on the Monaro or the Princes Highway, spare a thought for the men who marked out the boundary 150 years ago.

The Port Phillip District, which became Victoria in 1851, had as its northern and eastern boundary, "a straight line drawn from Cape Howe to the nearest source of the River Murray, and thence the course of that River to the eastern boundary of the Province of South Australia".

It sounds easy, but nothing is easy when the lawyers start to dig into it. For instance, who did the actual waters of the Murray belong to – Victoria or New South Wales? This was an important question. A lot of income came from taxes on river traffic. You guessed it: the river was retained by New South Wales. The precise boundary was defined as the highest point of the river bank on the southern (Victorian) side of the river.

This was put to the test in an extraordinary way years later, in 1980. Alexander Joseph Reed was fishing on the edge of the Murray near Echuca. Edward Donald Ward, from the top of the bank above, shot and killed him. Which State had jurisdiction, New South Wales or Victoria? The matter went through the Victorian courts but on appeal the High Court decided that although the shot was fired from Victoria (the top of the bank) the victim died in New South Wales (the bottom of the bank). Ward was re-tried in New South Wales and sentenced to life imprisonment.

Something of the same occurred here in Gippsland, though in a much more light-hearted way. Some years ago it was discovered that there was a slight error in marking the State border where it crosses the Princes Highway north of Genoa. The line was fixed fourteen metres further south than it should have been, with the result that for years and years the New South Wales Department of Main Roads had been repairing fourteen metres of highway that Victoria should have been looking after. One small win for Victoria!

The main point of this story is the surveying of 'the straight line drawn from Cape Howe to the nearest source of the River Murray' – the Gippsland-New South Wales border. The Cape Howe end of the line was relatively easy; it was the other end that posed difficulties. A surveyor named Thomas Scott Townsend had earlier been sent by the New

South Wales Surveyor-General (Thomas Mitchell, the famous explorer, no less!) to locate the spot. This was in the 1840s, long before the separation of Victoria.

Townsend was a very experienced surveyor. He laid out the street plans for Albury and Wagga; he surveyed and marked out the port facilities at Corner Inlet and Portland (then both still part of New South Wales); the second highest mountain in Australia – Mount Townsend – is named after him ... and he did indeed discover the 'nearest point' of the Murray to Cape Howe. This turned out to be a soakage fed by a natural spring in the shadow of Mount Kosciusko. (Does it surprise you to learn that Victoria extends to within three kilometres of the summit of Mount Kosciusko?) The place was later called Townsend Corner in his honour, though there's no actual corner there. Townsend's later life was less fortunate. He was held up by bushrangers, robbed, relieved of his trousers, and left tied up, hands behind his back, to the wheel of his coach – and the march flies were particularly bad at the time! He lost his reason towards the end of his life, was estranged from his family, and ended his life in a mental institution. We honour him, however, as one who contributed to the opening up of our land and the formation of our history.

Strangely, although the border was defined so precisely, nothing was done about it except that a pile of stones was placed near the actual point of Cape Howe. It wasn't until nearly thirty years after Townsend's location of the western end of the 'straight line' to the coast that the line was precisely marked out on the ground and on the maps.

That marking-out was the work of two government surveyors, Alexander Black and Alexander Allan, though they had a third surveyor, William Turton assisting them for part of the time. The line has ever since been known as the Black-Allan line. Black marked out the western third of the line, from the Murray eastward, while Allan was responsible for the eastern two-thirds of the line through to Cape Howe. The western section was clearly the most difficult, passing through the toughest country of the Australian Alps. A hundred creeks, gullies, and major rivers had to be crossed, some flowing north from Victoria into New South Wales and others returning the compliment. Dozens of men did the heavy work. Packhorses were used to carry stores and the heavy instruments required. There were frequent delays when fog or heavy rain obscured the sighting points needed to mark the line. The work started in 1870 and was completed two years later. It was a gigantic achievement.

Marking out the line with a series of cairns was hard enough. But calculating just where the line should go was a mathematical and surveying feat of the highest order. How should it be calculated? How do you make a 'straight line'? It's not just a matter of putting a ruler on the map and drawing a pencil line along it. A map is a flat surface. The ground is a curved surface. Over the 176 kilometre distance of the line, the earth's curvature is significant. Black and Allan used amazingly complicated mathematical geometry to plot the course of the line. Later calculations using modern computer and satellite technology confirmed their work to have been extraordinarily precise.

It was another ninety years, nearly, before anyone else walked the full distance of the line. A small party led by Keith McPherson made the trip. McPherson left a light-hearted account of their journey:

The trip took 19 days. We started out with five – three men and two women. When we reached the Bonang Highway, the first man said that his daughter was having a birthday so he went home. We had just left the next major road – the

Cann River Highway, when the next chap suddenly said, 'It's just one bloody ridge after another', so he turned around and went home. This left me, my wife Daphne, and one other woman (Bessie McCallum) *to go on to Cape Howe.*

The line was now scientifically established, but not yet set in law. Both legislatures – in New South Wales and Victoria – went to sleep on the matter. Perhaps the Ward murder of 1980 woke them up. The oversight was eventually rectified, but not until the next century! The Black-Allan line was proclaimed in the Government Gazettes of both States in February, 2006. A few days later the two State Governors, John Landy (Victoria) and Marie Bashir (New South Wales) met at Allan's Peg, the point where the line crosses the Delegate River, reached across the border, and shook hands to confirm the legal establishment of the border. A plaque was unveiled. The 300 people present applauded. One of the papers of the day commented that 130 years of a Clayton's Border – the border you have when you do not officially have a border – was brought to an end.

Alexander Black went straight from his achievement with Alexander Allan to take up a position as Acting District Surveyor at Bairnsdale, from where he was transferred shortly afterwards to Sale. He eventually became Surveyor-General of Victoria from 1886 to 1894.

So ... the next time you're driving round the coast, please take a little time to stop at the border. They've provided a place for you to pull in. You'll be able to read the plaque that's mounted on a small cairn. It records the achievements of Black and Allan and was placed there in September, 1985, as part of Victoria's 150th anniversary commemorations.

The Loss of the *Trinculo*

Dozens of vessels have gone down along the Gippsland coast and hundreds of lives have been lost. One of the worst tragedies was the sinking of the *Glenelg*, an iron-built steam-driven schooner, in deep water off Lakes Entrance in 1900. Thirty-eight people drowned, while three crew members escaped in a lifeboat before the ship went down. What deeds of heroism occurred in the last moments of the ship we shall never know.

In other cases we know the details of the last moments and can pay tribute to the heroism shown by the crew members. The sinking of the *Trinculo* is an example. This took place much earlier, in 1869. The *Trinculo* was a three-masted, timber-built barque, named after a figure in Shakespeare's play, *The Tempest*. I can't understand how a ship could be named for a character in a play about a shipwreck! However, *The Tempest* has a happy ending, and so too has our tale, though not before a final scene of incredible drama and bravery.

The *Trinculo*, of 300 tons and with a crew of ten, was trading around the Australian coastline. Her final journey was from Newcastle in New South Wales to Albany in Western Australia, carrying coal, and she was on the return journey when the disaster occurred. She was carrying no cargo, just ballast. The only passengers were the wife of the ship's captain and their sixteen-month-old son.

The ship met strong south-easterly winds and huge waves – a tempest! – off the Ninety Mile Beach. She took so much water Captain Williams decided to beach her. She ran head on in to the beach, but almost immediately swung broadside on, which spelt the vessel's doom. She settled into the sand only thirty yards or so from the shore.

But still, the surf was so rough and the undertow so strong that all hands could have been lost so near and yet so far to safety. Here, a stunning demonstration of skill and courage took place. One of the crew, Thomas Lefevre, apparently acting on his own initiative, grabbed the log-line – the rope tied with knots at regular intervals and used for measuring the speed of the ship at sea – dived into the water and somehow succeeded in reaching the shore.

A heavier line was attached to the log-line and hauled to the shore, enabling the rest of the rescue attempts to be made with somewhat more confidence. There was nothing on the beach to attach the line to. Lefevre, and later with others to help him, simply stood on the beach holding the line tight while those on board the vessel one by one attempted to get to shore by means of this single strand. First one or two of the crew members who could swim went ashore, all safely. Next it was the turn of those who could not swim. This was a desperate manoeuvre as if they had lost hold of the line they could well have been crushed in the surf or swept out to sea in the undertow. Again, however, they survived.

Now came the most perilous of the rescue attempts. The captain's wife, Mrs Williams, was next to take to the water. She was unconscious and black in the face on reaching shore, but was dragged on to the beach and resuscitated – with the aid, a little later, of a hot cup of tea. (How they managed to bring tea from the wreck I can't understand!)

But Mrs Williams' infant son was still on board, with his father. The child was strapped to his father's back by the remaining crew members, and the pair launched themselves into the surf Almost immediately Captain Williams was crashed on to his back by the force of the breakers. The little boy took the full weight of his father against the bottom and was knocked insensible. Still, they managed to reach shore. It was thought the boy was dead, but, again, like his mother, he was revived.

The last of the sailors reached shore safely. Still, their situation was known to no one and they were far from any settlement. It was two days before help arrived from Peter Clement's Prospect Station near Seaspray. The mother and child were first taken there and the whole party eventually returned to Melbourne.

Two matters of note took place following the disaster. A marine court of inquiry was held to examine responsibility for the wreck. After very brief deliberations and hearing from few witnesses, the Court held that the cause of the wreck was entirely one of misfortune. No one was to blame. The seaworthiness of the vessel was not investigated. Some believed it was a whitewash.

Three months later, at the prompting of the newspapers of the day, the Humane Society of Victoria awarded Thomas Lefevre a Silver Medal for bravery. The Governor, the Marquess of Normandy, newly arrived from Britain and British to his bootstraps, presented Lefevre's medal in a ceremony at the Melbourne Town Hall. The Governor extolled Lefevre's bravery. 'It showed,' he said, 'what could be done by the pluck, skill, and determination of the British sailor.'

Even when he has a French name, we're tempted to add!

The *Trinculo* still rests in the sands of the Ninety Mile Beach, or at least its iron frame is there. Drive out from Seaspray and you'll find it a few kilometres before Golden Beach. There's something very poignant about the remains of this once vibrant vessel. As you stand there, you can easily imagine the crashing of the surf and the cries from the ship as Thomas Lefevre dived into the breakers on that March morning 150 years ago. And if you feel more than usually troubled in spirit as you walk along the beach it may be it's because you're walking over the grave of another vessel, now completely hidden under the sand. This is the *Paynesville*, a small local vessel that, extraordinarily, met its fate at this very spot just two years after the *Trinculo*.

But watch the weather! Trinculo may have the last laugh on you:

Here's neither bush nor shrub, he says in Shakespeare's play, *to bear off any weather at all, and another storm brewing; I hear it sing i' the wind; yond same black cloud,* *yond huge one, looks like a foul bumbard* that would shed its liquor ...*

*_Bumbard_ (obsolete): an early form of cannon.

The Saving of Walhalla

'Burn! Burn! Burn! Burn!'

The chant rises as the flames begin to take hold. A dozen men, their heads wrapped in scarves, not from the cold but from fear of the infection, encircle the building.

'Burn, you bastard! Burn!' one man shouts.

The dreaded time has come. Smallpox has arrived. Melbourne has already suffered terribly. Forty and more have died there. The miners of Walhalla have fought hard to keep the invader at bay, but to no avail, it seems. But can something be salvaged? Can the damage be limited to this one case?

The men are determined to make it so.

The year was 1869, and the victim was Sarah Jones. Her marriage became her requiem. Immediately after her wedding in Melbourne, Sarah returned to Walhalla with her husband, Will Hanks, a local miner. A celebration was held in their honour. It took little for the folk of Walhalla to find cause for a celebration. Will and Sarah virtually stepped out of the coach into the hotel.

The Grand Junction Hotel dominated the town. Recently built, it stood where the two streams of Stringers Creek converged. People gathered to honour the young couple, and the drinks flowed freely. But a cloud descended, even as the merriment was in full swing. Sarah became ill. Dr Hadden was sent for. One look was enough. Sarah was fevered; her body ached; her face was blistered.

Shocked, Hadden still sought confirmation. His colleague, James Boone, had served in a smallpox hospital in the States. He would know. Boone arrived to give a final judgment. There was no doubt. Sarah was in the deep grip of smallpox.

Henry Hadden took over. Under his strong direction, the people of the town, acted in unity as never before. The hotel was isolated. Sarah was removed to a back room. Only Henry Hadden had access to her. The miners drifted back to work, their heavy tread and strong language muted as they passed by the hotel, up and down the valley.

For days the situation hung in the balance. Will Hanks could stand it no longer. In the dead of night, he forced the window of his wife's room and carried her through the silent street to his cottage three hundred metres higher up the creek. Hanks's small son was a third occupant of the doomed house.

The men of Walhalla were angered but not dismayed. A paling fence was built, virtually in a day, around Hanks's shack. It was a gesture of defiance against the unseen enemy as much as a barrier to anyone coming near. Again, only Doctor Hadden was allowed to pass through.

For some days more, the patient hung on. Dr Hadden soothed her skin with cooling unguents; he brought water to her cracked lips; he treated her sores as best he could. But his efforts were unavailing. Sarah died on the seventh day.

The funeral must take place immediately. However, the cemetery is at the end of the town, and the narrow valley allows of only one road – through the middle of the settlement. To carry the body through the centre of town is unthinkable in view of the possible spread of the contagion. Sarah's body is sealed. She is carried to the brow of the small rise behind the place where she died, and is buried deep in the earth, consecrated not by church blessing but by the will and prayers of the people. Her grave was recently re-discovered. Stones of the valley, carefully placed, now serve as her tombstone.

But this is not the end of the story. The ad hoc anti-smallpox committee decreed that Hanks's cottage must be destroyed. Hanks himself moved into quarantine at the top end of the valley, and his house with everything in it was consigned to the flames.

That's where the story began.

'Burn! Burn! Burn! Burn!'

The house did burn. And all lingering traces of the smallpox scourge burnt with it. Walhalla was saved.

****

Dr Henry Hadden may well be regarded as the town's saviour. He himself has his own poignant story.

Early in life he was known as William Hadden. That was during his growing up and medical training in Ireland. Out here, he preferred to be known as Henry. Perhaps he wanted to cover something in his past. His past was certainly not without blemish. In Castlemaine, where he once worked, a woman was brought for childbirth. His bungling, apparently due to his intoxication, led to the death of both mother and child. Hadden was charged with medical negligence and served a term in prison. He came to Gippsland to rebuild his career, first to Omeo and then to Walhalla. The sad case of Sarah Hanks provided him with that opportunity, and he rose superbly to the occasion.

Several months later, Hadden visited Melbourne and returned just as the newly-weds, Will and Sarah Hanks, had done just a short time before.

His coach pursued its usual way, stopping at the several little settlements en route. At the Bunyip River all seemed to be well. At Crossover, the next stop, after the other passengers had alighted, Hadden was found propped in his seat, dead. How could this be?

The consensus was that he had fallen victim to his old drinking problem and his body reached some crisis point just there, in those strange circumstances. Perhaps his heart suddenly gave way. Hadden's body was interred at Shady Creek not far away. He lies there in solitude, in unhallowed ground, like Sarah Hanks with whose name and fate he will always be linked. His grave is there to this day, neatly fenced around by those who own the land.

Harmers Haven

This story is about Eddie Harmer … and a good deal more. The story is set in Wonthaggi in the hard days before and during the Great Depression.

Black coal had been found and mined in South Gippsland for decades. Privately-owned mines at Cape Paterson, Jumbunna, Korumburra, Outtrim, Kilcunda, and even as far afield as Coalville and Boolarra, had been worked since the 1850s. Falling returns, exacerbated by miners' strikes, resulted in the State looking to establish its own mine. Coal was needed for the great network of rail lines then in operation, all needing good quality black coal for their steam engines. If Victoria couldn't supply it, then it would have to be brought in from New South Wales at great cost to the State (and loss of colonial pride!)

The result was the establishment of the State Coalmine at Wonthaggi in 1909 and the resultant growth of a mining town, Wonthaggi, close by. Those familiar with the beginnings of Yallourn in the 1920s would understand the pattern. The rail line was extended from Nyora. Wonthaggi prospered. Within a few years the tent-city of the first miners had developed into a thriving town with all the facilities of other long-established towns in the region - *and a strong and militant Union organisation.* You could describe early Wonthaggi as a Union town. The Communist Party had a strong following.

You might think that the Government would see to it that conditions in its own mines were above board. Sadly, that was not the case. Technically, mining methods were first-class, even world-leading. But for the men working in them, old and back-breaking methods were still the norm – pit-ponies, canaries in cages, narrow drives, hot and humid conditions, and long hours – five and a half day weeks and two weeks' annual leave. The pay was good for some, but payment was by each man's individual production, which led to inequalities and industrial problems.

Then there were the accidents. The safety record of the Wonthaggi mines was appalling. I've been looking at a list of the fatal accidents that occurred. In the period, 1910 to 1938, sixty-nine men lost their lives in mining accidents. There were several multiple deaths. The worst tragedy was on the 15 February, 1937. Thirteen men, mostly team leaders, had gone underground to investigate the facts behind the workers' complaints. A strike meeting of 500 men was being held in town at the very moment a huge explosion occurred in No 20 shaft. There are many graphic accounts of what happened. The most gripping is by Philip Harper in his excellent book, *The Wonthaggi Coalfields*. Harper's father was one of those killed.

The morning of Monday February 15th, 1937, was a day in my life which I shall never forget. A hot north wind was blowing across the flat Powlett River plains and the nearby coastal sand dunes. The effect of the explosion on the Township was quite dramatic. ... When the news was flashed through to the Township there was a wild scatter of men and equipment towards the No 20 Shaft Mine, to offer assistance in whatever way possible.'

Dozens of men immediately volunteered to go down in the hope of rescue, but nothing could be done. A Royal Commission investigated the disaster and found that the cause was one of the men lighting a naked flame which had ignited deadly methane gas. The widows were granted £2 a week and safety improvements were recommended.

Alongside these terrible happenings the miners and their families mostly lived wretched lives, particularly during the Depression years. Reduced wages and a series of protracted strikes made things worse. The writings of Wendy Lowenstein have brilliantly exposed the harrowing experiences of the miners' families, while the linocuts of the renowned artist, Noel Counihan, brought home the miners' appalling working conditions.

However a magnificent informal system of mateship and mutual support developed. Some of the miners and their families began to spend their precious weekends and holidays at Wreck Beach, seven or eight kilometres from Wonthaggi. The foreshore was unoccupied and neglected. The men gathered driftwood, kerosene tins, and old timber to build rough shelters for themselves behind the sand dunes, where they could stay for days on end. Some put up tents left over from the original miners' camp. They organised beach sports and picnics; they ate and drank together; they caught rabbits and fish; they gloried in the bracing air so much in contrast to the hot and fetid conditions they experienced underground. Eddie Harmer and his family were amongst them.

During these savage days of the Depression, retrenchments, strikes, and resultant lockouts meant the miners were without pay for months on end. Some lost their homes. The unofficial settlement at Wreck Bay became a refuge. Many lived there permanently. Some were young men who were laid off when reaching twenty-one due to the pernicious practice of sacking them to avoid paying adult wages. The 'settlers' at the coast began supplying food rations to their Union brothers in town.

A good deal later, in the 1950s, the Wreck Beach miners' community took on renewed life. With unofficial Communist Party backing and support from the wider Union movement, a large parcel of land was bought and blocks made available to individual miners and their families. They put up cheap but permanent houses and a strong feeling of brotherhood and common purpose developed. Jack McLeod, the local Communist Party organiser, and Eddie Harmer, head of the Wonthaggi Miners Union were two of the leaders. They came up with the name, 'Harmers' Haven' for the place and it stuck – though many people since have referred to it as 'Commies' Corner'. They weren't far wrong!

Eddie Harmer was a superb Union leader. He'd been sent out from England as a young boy under one of the Empire settlement schemes of those times. He knew every inch of the miners' life. He, himself, was unemployed for several years in the mid-'thirties. In negotiations with the government he was firm but respectful. His maxim was, 'What the majority want, that's what we'll do. In the mines, the majority always decides.' Someone who was present at his funeral at the Wonthaggi Cemetery one windy day in 1990 told me of the poignant scene as Eddie's life story was told to the little gathering while in the background the old places of furious activity, where mateship was the watchword of the day, where Eddie's lifeblood was spilt, stood, now mouldering into the landscape of time and place.

There's no place in Gippsland like Harmers Haven. The old buildings have gone, but the spirit remains. In Wonthaggi itself, reminders of the roaring days of mining are everywhere around you. Even the old mine whistle still blows each day. Here at Harmers Haven you don't have physical reminders of the past, but if you know the history of the place when you come and if you're receptive to it, you'll *feel* the spirit of the past. It will grip you. And you might hear the shouts of the children at play and see the smoke drifting up from the campfires as the ghosts of Eddie Harmer and Jack McLeod and the others live and laugh their time away, still snubbing their noses at the government and the bosses and the whole wretched system that once sought to enslave them. They're free now. They always were, really.

The Story of an Island

This is the story of an island. It's a beautiful island, small enough to know intimately – and it belongs to you! Go and visit it if you can, but if you can't do that, find the 1973 film, *Summerfield*, on your computer and watch it. It's set on the island, and is an excellent film (though don't let the children watch it with you!)

Churchill Island clings to the larger Phillip Island like a baby leaning on its mother's breast. In Victoria's history, it is celebrated as the place where our soil was first turned over in agricultural enterprise. The first garden in Gippsland was planted here in 1801 by Lieutenant James Grant, and that story is told elsewhere in this volume. The Boonwurrung people had been summer visitors to the island for aeons before that, but they didn't plant gardens. They came for the shellfish and mutton birds and fattened up for the leaner winter months to come.

The first real touch of Europeanisation was the granting of a pastoral lease to John Rogers over a group of small islands in Westernport Bay, including Churchill Island.

That was in 1854. The island's ensuing history is well-known. The Friends of Churchill Island have published copiously about it. Rebecca Sanders wrote a PhD on the island in 2015. To cut a long story short, Rogers first leased, then bought the island. He had possession of the place for eighteen years, until 1872, although during that time the Pickersgill family lived there and raised a large family. The precise nature of the relationship between Rogers' tenure and the Pickersgills' occupation is the subject of continuing debate. For our purposes, we might pay tribute to both parties. They both lived there; they both farmed the land; they both, surely, fell under the island's spell.

Rogers makes a good case study of a knockabout Gippslander in those more heady days. He came out from Helston in Cornwall in 1839, aged twenty-five. Rogers found a different life out here. He began by looking for land in East Gippsland before turning to farming near where Lang Lang is today. Then he went off to the Bendigo diggings and spent some time in New Zealand before gaining the lease of Churchill Island. He was then forty years of age. In 1872, after those eighteen years, Rogers sold out and went off to Brandy Creek, then known as Buln

Buln, where he selected land. John Rogers ended up one of the most prominent citizens of West Gippsland. Truly, a remarkable story of initiative and endeavour.

Churchill Island passed to J D McHaffie, the pioneer of Phillip Island, and he on-sold to Samuel Amess. This is where the modern history of Churchill Island begins. It also marks the beginning of the island turning more towards Melbourne than its Gippsland hinterland. It is now to be seen more as an outlier of Melbourne and of Western District money than being of Gippsland in origin and spirit. The island is solidly in Gippsland, but unique in its style. Nowhere else in Gippsland is a bit like Churchill Island.

Samuel Amess was a leading citizen of Melbourne. As a builder, he rode the golden boom of the 1850s. He erected substantial buildings such as the Treasury Building, the old Exchange Building, the Customs House, the Kew Asylum, the Government Printing Office, the original General Post Office, and many railway stations, including Ballarat. He was Mayor of Melbourne at the time of the opening of the Town Hall. He paid privately for the festivities associated with its opening, including a Fancy Dress Ball, attended by

3,000 people who dined on boars' heads, sucking pigs, jellies, and champagne.

Amess built the substantial house – Amess House – that now stands as the centrepiece of Churchill Island. Christine Grayden, Curator of the Heritage Farm, has put together an amazing document about Amess and his life in Melbourne and on the island. She tells how Amess entertained constantly and liberally. The Visitors Book is a list of the Melbourne A-Graders of the time. "A sweet little Eden on earth bright as day", wrote one. Another entry reads, "Have seen the Old Year out and the New Year in at Churchill and now think that if always spent on the island life would really be worth living". And another, "Churchill is a delightful place such a one as the Emperor of Russia would envy".

Amess extended the gardens already established by John Rogers. He turned the two small cottages into outbuildings of the main house. As to the house itself, one visitor described it as "a comfortable rural villa ... with ample accommodation for any number of visitors". The house is the centre of attraction today. It is furnished and decorated as in its original dispensation. In the garden stands the one-and-only gesture of showmanship – a cannon from a nineteenth-century warship. This cannon has been the cause of furious debate over the years. Amess himself gave credence to the fact that it came from the American vessel, the *Shenandoah*, which put into Melbourne at the time of the American Civil War. That understanding has now been utterly demolished. Another suggestion is that the cannon was a gift from a noted resident of Phillip Island, Captain John Cleeland (celebrated as the owner of the Melbourne Cup winner, Wollomai). Today, most visitors to the house head straight for the cannon! Amess imported a fold of West Highland cattle from his native Scotland, and, as an active member of the Acclimatisation Society, released exotic rabbits, quail, and pheasants on his land.

All told, there is a harmony between the gracious feeling of Amess House as it is today and the kindly and benevolent figure of Samuel Amess himself. The house continued in the possession of the family, over three generations, until 1929 – a span of fifty-seven years: one year for every hectare of the island! The Amess-Churchill Island story ends sadly. The great-grandson of the original Samuel was forced to sell the island after being found guilty of embezzlement and given a prison sentence.

For the next six years, from 1929 to 1935, Churchill Island was held by Gerald Buckley, a Western District grazier. He never lived here, but had many improvements made by his managers, the Jeffery brothers. As against the former use of the land solely as a leisure retreat, the brothers built up an eighty-strong dairy herd. The milk and cream were carried to the mainland by horse and cart at low-tide, when the narrow crossing was useable.

After Buckley's death, a Collins Street dentist, Harry Jenkins, bought the island. Jenkins was more than a dentist. He was a supreme adventurer. He returned from the First World War and, alongside his dental practice, took up motor-racing. Then, in 1931 he travelled to England, bought a tiny two-seater aeroplane with a friend, Harold Jeffrey, and flew it back to Melbourne in dozens of tiny hops, stopping over in Calcutta (Kolkata) to join a tiger hunt. Jenkins' son, Ted was a paraplegic. He lived on the island, cared for by several staff members, including a nursing sister, Margaret Campbell. This was the situation for nearly thirty years, until both Ted and his father died and the island was left to the faithful servant, Sister Margaret

Sister Margaret carried on for a further ten years. She was known with great fondness in the Phillip Island community. Advancing frailty made her give up the island and it passed to a Melbourne businessman, Alex Classou, who had ideas of establishing a horse stud, but by then a campaign was underway to secure the island for the community. With the strong support of the Premier, Sir Rupert Hamer, Churchill Island was bought with public funds by the Victoria Conservation Trust. Over the years the island has been run by the Friends of Phillip Island Society (FOCIS) with enormous voluntary help from other people in the local community.

Churchill Island belongs to you. Enjoy it!

Frontier Justice

There's an intriguing and tragic story in our early Gippsland history. It involves early Tasmania, then known as Van Diemen's Land, the infant city of Melbourne, and the sandy coastal area of South Gippsland.

The story begins in Van Diemen's Land. In the 1820s and 30s, as settlers spread into the interior, they were met with resistance from the aboriginal inhabitants. Some terrible things occurred, culminating in the 'Black War' where armed men tried to drive the aboriginal population completely out of their island home. The attempt failed, but it left the survivors hugely reduced in numbers and separated from their ancestral lands.

One man who did something to protect them was George Augustus Robinson. He persuaded a remnant of fifteen or sixteen blacks to leave the island and travel with him to Melbourne to make a new start. From what we now know about the attachment of aboriginal folk to their land, it was bound to fail. Robinson did what he could – he had now become the official Protector of Aborigines in the Port

Phillip District – but these survivors became a bedraggled and pitiful group living on handouts, rejected and heartsore.

This story concerns five members of this group: two men, Tunnerminnerwait and Maulboyheenner, and three women, Pyterruner, Planobeener, and Truganini. You might have heard of Truganini. She's widely believed to have been the last full-blooded Tasmanian aborigine, and a lot has been written about her. Her early life reveals something of the murderous treatment meted out to the aborigines. Prior to her removal to Melbourne, she had seen her mother killed by sailors, her sister abducted by sealers, and the man to whom she was promised in marriage murdered by some timber-cutters who then raped her.

However, our attention is fixed on the two men, Tunnerminnerwait and Maulboyheener. Tunnerminnerwait agreed to go with Robinson on a tour of the Western District, where it was hoped he would be able to help bring blacks and whites into some kind of peaceful co-existence. The scheme backfired entirely. Tunnerminnerwait returned to Melbourne inflamed by the savage treatment meted out to the blacks, especially at Portland Bay. The results of his experience were soon to be seen.

Tunnerminnerwait rejoined his four companions. Carefully they put together a cache of weapons, including guns and ammunition. They began to raid settlers living on the outskirts of the town. From their hideouts in the bush they raided isolated settlers, stole weapons, killed cattle, and burned down buildings. This was more than an attempt to live freely in the bush. It was a campaign of revenge on their white 'enemy', a war if you like. A reverse 'Black War'. The party drifted out as far as Dandenong, southwards to Westernport, then drifted eastward along the coast, reaching as far as Wilson's Promontory. One aboriginal woman who has studied their escapade believes they were trying desperately to find a way back to Van Diemen's Land, the land of their birth and their dreaming.

Turning westward, again, at Cape Paterson, they came upon a group of whalers. Some believe that Truganini recognised one man as one of her abusers of many years earlier. Shots were exchanged. Two of the whalers were shot dead. These were the first white people to be physically harmed during the several months of the campaign. Now a major attempt was undertaken to capture the 'marauders'. Twice, police parties failed. The third, with the aid of native trackers, succeeded. The five were captured and transported to Melbourne where they were placed in the Old Melbourne Gaol. Pentridge was yet to be built.

At their trial for murder, the five defendants were represented by Redmond Barry, the same man who forty years later, as Justice Sir Redmond Barry, would sentence Ned Kelly to be hanged. Barry tried hard to save the five. He requested that half of the jury be made up of aboriginal people, and also that the two men be allowed to testify in their own defence. Mr Justice Willis refused both applications. As non-citizens and as non-Christians these men had no rights under the law. This was a white community and it was against this community that the offences had been committed. The white community would decide the matter. The jury took just thirty minutes to reach its decision.

The women were freed; the two men were sentenced to death. The jury asked for clemency. This appeal was duly sent to Sydney, where the Executive Council of New South Wales rejected it. Three weeks later, a rough gallows was erected. The two victims, clothed in white were driven to the scene by horse and dray. Six thousand citizens crammed every vantage point to witness the ghastly last moments of these two black 'freedom fighters'. Their bodies were buried not within the Melbourne Cemetery, but outside it. The Victoria Market stands there today.

The date was Thursday, twentieth of January, 1842. These were the first executions to be held in Victoria. The Port Phillip Herald commented that there was no doubt about the justness of the sentence, and that the execution of the two aborigines was the imperative duty of the authorities to vindicate the impartiality of British law.

Each year on the anniversary of the executions, people gather at the scaffold site to mourn the men's death. In 2016 a permanent memorial was erected on the site, the corner of Victoria and Franklin Streets. It is imaginatively designed. The memorial stone bears just two words: *Tunnerminnerwait* and *Maulboyheenner*.

The Snells of West Gippsland

Gippsland is famous for its scenery, its greenery, its history, its mystery, but to the world of a hundred years ago, Gippsland was best known to the world, not for these things, but for the remarkable Snell Family.

It's a strange story – of how an enterprising family found fame and fortune by drawing on the single resource they possessed: that of the sheer size of the family. Not of the whole family together, but of the individual size of three of its members, Clara, Tom, and Anna.

William and Elizabeth Snell were amongst Bunyip's early settlers. They had come out from Exeter in England in the early 1870s and established a dairy farm north of Bunyip, but William was also a baker and opened a shop on the Old Sale Road at Bunyip North. The parents themselves were of normal build – and so were the children, except for those three, Clara, Tom, and Anna. Their career began in 1886 when the management of the Waxworks Museum in Melbourne heard of the extraordinary size of the three children.

In those days people would flock to all sorts of exhibitions of curious or sensational things. At the Waxworks Museum, beside the wax figures of historical characters like Napoleon and Shakespeare, the museum specialised in its Chamber of Horrors showing axe-killings and other macabre scenes. Live exhibitions were particularly popular. The Chinese Giant, Cheng Wu, caused a sensation, and so did Australia's Tom Thumb, John Armstrong. In the same way, crowds flocked to the Museum when Clara, Tom, and Anna Snell appeared. They were mere children then. A photograph taken in Melbourne at the time shows the girls standing leviathan-like, arms bared, with Tom, lying, bare-chested, like Tarzan, on a rug in front of them.

Two years later, the family was on show in England, first in the Snells' place of origin, Exeter, and then on a national tour of the major cities. A cigarette card was produced, featuring 'Clara Snell, the Largest Woman in the World, on Show at Barnum's Circus'. An English newspaper wrote:

The eldest and most remarkable of the giant children is Clara Elizabeth, who stands 5 feet 9 inches [175 cm] in height, weighs 28 stone 6 lbs [181 kg] and measures 66 inches [168 cm] round the waist. ... Her "little" brother,

Thomas Snell, aged 10 years, stands 5 feet 1 inch [155 cm]*'in height, and weighs 13 stone 2 lbs* [83 kg], *while Anna, an 8-year-old sister, is but 4 feet 6 inches* [137 cm] *in height, yet turns the scale at 12 stone 2 lbs* [77 kg].

The Snell exhibition toured Australia twice to great crowds, penetrating to outback places like Rockhampton and Mount Morgan, and also to faraway Western Australia. They exhibited in a number of cities in Europe, and then across the United States. Other tours took them around New Zealand and also to South Africa. It was said in various newspaper reports that the 'Australian Giants' had done more to advertise and promote Australia to the world than highly-paid commissioners and diplomats.

The children were in perfectly good health. In time Clara grew to 40 stone (254 kg), Tom to 25 stone (159 kg), and Anna 28 stone (178 kg). When exhibited, the children would sometimes sing and play the piano. The whole family was very musical. The children were light on their feet and loved dancing.

William Snell, the father, was an enthusiastic promoter. When, for instance, he read in Sydney's 'World's News' of an English heavyweight, he wrote to the paper:

Having seen in your paper an account of the heavyweight
girl from Yorkshire, I beg to enclose some particulars of
my own family which I think will be of interest as showing
here in Australia we can challenge the world.

Mr Snell went on to give the dimensions of the three
children. The Warragul Guardian wryly commented:

It has been quite a common thing for Gippslanders to
expatiate on the immense growth of their trees and scrub,
but it has remained for Mr Snell to demonstrate the
fattening qualities of the district in connection with human
nature.

Clara and Anna continued to tour for many years. Tom,
however, was not so keen and pulled out of the show when
he turned twenty-one. He worked hard, particularly with
the axe and managed to reach normal size. He moved to
Nar Nar Goon, married Harriet Maskell at St John's
Church, and ran the grocer's shop in town. He later lived in
Tynong and died in 1949, aged seventy-two. He is buried
in the Bunyip Cemetery.

The two girls, Clara and Anna, however, continued to tour,
apparently with their enthusiasm undiminished. Locally

they were subject to snide comments, like this piece in the Warragul Guardian:

Miss Clara Snell ... had a narrow escape from being bitten by a snake the other day. While out in one of the paddocks the young lady observed a lizard disappear under a small log and, without thinking, gave the log a kick, when a snake emerged from under it and made for her. Miss Snell turned and ran, and when the snake had followed her for a few yards, and perhaps perceived what it was running at, it also turned tail and left. Evidently 35 stone was too much for it to tackle.

The sisters experienced problems wherever they went. When travelling by train they would sit in the guard's van with its double doors, the carriage doors being too narrow for them. When going about the countryside, for instance to a dance, they used a dray. A normal buggy could not carry them. Despite these difficulties they continued to tour and built up quite a fortune for themselves. True to their roots, they retired to run the Robin Hood Hotel at Drouin West, where their parents were now living. Anna married (a man named Small!), but Clara remained unmarried.

Anna died, aged 54, in 1930, without much public comment. By then she had slipped out of public view. The earlier death of Clara from liver cancer in 1914, however, attracted notices around the country:

DEATH OF GIPPSLAND GIANTESS

One of the oldest natives of the Bunyip district, Miss Clara Snell, died at Nar Nar Goon on Saturday ... There was a very large attendance at the funeral on Monday. It was the expressed wish of deceased that her remains should be carried to their last resting place in the spring cart in which she used to travel about the country when on tour. The hearse travelled in front of the funeral, and was filled with wreaths. The spring cart with the remains followed. It took 6 men, including the brother of deceased, to carry the remains to the grave. The coffin was lowered into the grave by eight men with a double set of four ropes ... The large banner which did duty as an advertising sign for the Snell family was buried with the remains.

Members of the Snell family still live around Gippsland, and you occasionally come across snippets of news and information about the famous trio. Just recently, I noticed a paragraph in an old paper from a local who had grown up

65

with the Snell children. 'One of our great boasts as children,' she wrote, 'was that we could always see the Snells for nothing but our cousins at South Yarra actually had to pay to see them at the waxworks'.

The Victoria Cross

Two men associated with Gippsland have won the Victoria Cross for gallantry. Neither was a born-and-bred local boy. However, one was living in Leongatha when he enlisted and the other ended his life here, tragically, in Boolarra.

Walter John Peeler ('Wally') was a Castlemaine boy, but when he married Emma Hewitt, both aged nineteen, they set up home in Leongatha and it was from there that Wally enlisted in the 1st AIF. That was in 1916 and by then they had two little children. As a Lance-Corporal in the 3rd Pioneer Battalion machine gun section, he took part in the Passchendaele Offensive on the Western Front. On 4 October, 1917, during an attack on the heavily defended German line, he displayed extraordinary skill and bravery. When the advancing Australian troops met heavy fire from a shell-hole, Peeler rushed the position across open territory and cleared out the enemy single-handed. Twice more on the same day he performed similar acts of bravery. In all he personally accounted for thirty of the enemy. His citation for the VC concluded, 'He displayed an absolute fearlessness in making his way ahead of the first wave of the assault, and the fine example which he set ensured the success of the attack against most determined opposition'.

Peeler was later badly wounded and invalided home. On his discharge he and his family moved to Bairnsdale. He was a fine cricketer and in 1922 represented Bairnsdale at Country Week cricket. His marriage to Emma failed and he remarried. When the Second World War broke out, Peeler put his age down and re-enlisted. He served in the Middle East and then in the Dutch East Indies where he was captured and spent three and a half years in a Japanese prisoner-of war camp. When the Shrine of Remembrance was completed in 1934 he served as the first custodian of the Shrine, a post he retained for the next thirty years (with time out for his WW2 service!) Some record!

Maurice Vincent Buckley was, after Captain Albert Jacka, probably Australia's most celebrated VC winner of the First World War. He was quite a different kettle of fish to Jacka – and to Wally Peeler. Buckley was 'a dare-devil and a bit of a larrikin' in the words of a member of his family. He enlisted in the 13 Light Horse, 1st AIF, very soon after the War began and sailed to base camp in Egypt. Here his war ended – for a time. In Cairo he became badly infected with both gonorrhea and syphilis and was shipped home as medically unfit. At Langwarrin on the Mornington Peninsula, a camp was set up for VD patients and military recalcitrants, and Buckley was sent here. However, he decamped after four months and was declared AWL. The civil and military police were unable to find him and he was officially struck off the army roll.

After two months, however, he turned up in Sydney, at the recruitment office, and re-enlisted. Whether he wished to redeem himself or whether he missed the army life or whether he was short of money or simply wanted to serve his country is unclear. All these motives have been suggested, although within the family, they say that his re-enlistment was a family decision. They calculated that the last place the military police would look for a deserter was within its own ranks! He now enlisted under a false name. He took his deceased younger brother's first name and his mother's maiden name and enlisted as 'Gerald Sexton' and served under that name until his moment of glory occurred. No one picked up his gambit.

He was not quite a reformed character, however. He went AWL for brief periods on several occasions, although, once in the front line he showed enough courage and ability to be promoted through the ranks, eventually becoming

Sergeant Gerald Sexton. Sexton was drafted into the 13th Battalion, 4th Brigade under the general command of John Monash. Amongst other bitter engagements the Battalion took part in the disastrous 1st Battle of Bullecourt in April, 1917, where the Australians suffered 3289 casualties, including 1166 taken prisoner. Sexton was amongst the survivors.

On 8 August, 1918, the Allies began the final offensive against the German front line that would see them through to victory in November. On that day, Sexton was in charge of a machine-gun section of the 13th Battalion. When his section suddenly came under heavy fire, "Sexton stood up in full view of the enemy, calmly noted the position of the gun from the flashes, and, firing from the hip, put it out of action". Thus read his citation for a Distinguished Conduct Medal (DCM), which was duly awarded.

A few weeks later, on 18 September, came the action that won Sexton his Victoria Cross. In the attack on the German-held town of Le Verguier, confronted by entrenched enemy machine-gun posts, Sexton ran across open ground amidst a hail of bullets, firing his Lewis gun from the hip, wild-west style, and put all three enemy posts out of action. Many Germans were killed and thirty taken prisoner, including a battalion commander. The Victoria Cross was awarded because of his "most conspicuous bravery".

It was now that Sexton revealed his true identity. His DCM and VC were presented in May, 1919 by King George V under his real name of Maurice Vincent Buckley. His earlier misdemeanours were quickly forgotten. He was lionised by the public on his return home. Buckley was a Catholic, and John Wren, that staunch Catholic wheeler-dealer, took Buckley under his wing. They travelled together to Western Australia, and later Wren staked Buckley in a business venture in road construction.

This is what brought Maurice Buckley to Gippsland ... and to his death. Buckley and his business partner, another of Wren's protégés, won a contract with the Country Roads Board to carry out work on the Morwell River Road between Boolarra and Gunyah. Three weeks into the contract, on 21 January, 1921, Buckley arrived in Boolarra after a hard day's work on horseback, tied up the horse (a 'pony') near the railway crossing and went off for a drink. What happened next is clouded in contradictory accounts. I'll take the report of the inquest into Buckley's death as the true story. This read as follows:

Edmund Kay Penaluna, dairy-farmer of Boolarra said, "On the evening of January 15 I was sitting with Sgt. Buckley outside the Railway Hotel, Boolarra. A young man named Ryan came up with the horse Buckley used to ride. The latter said to him, "Put him over the railway gates," and Ryan said, "I'll have a try." The horse refused twice to jump and Ryan fell off. Buckley then called out, "Let me have a go of it," and put the horse at the gates. It refused to jump and baulked. Buckley tried again and this time fell off, and his head struck the hard metal road.'

The inquest went on to hear that Buckley seemed to be unhurt, got up, remounted, and cantered off along the Gunyah Road. That evening he was found by a local family lying unconscious on the roadside. Mounted Policeman Edwards was called from Boolarra. Buckley was transferred to Mount St Evins Hospital in Melbourne, where he died six days later without regaining consciousness. He was twenty-nine.

Buckley's death occasioned a huge outpouring of public grief. Newspapers around the nation told of the tragedy on the Gunyah Road. After a Requiem Mass at St Patrick's Cathedral, the coffin was carried on a gun carriage through streets lined six deep with mourners to the Brighton

Cemetery. Ten Victoria Cross winners were pall-bearers, including Albert Jacka and Walter Peeler.

The story of Maurice Buckley's life and death constitute a grim but glorious tale of selfless service, of tragedy, of folly and redemption. In the court of public opinion he was adjudged a hero. In the bar of the Railway Hotel, Boolarra, there is no doubt he would pass the pub test! I think, to Maurice Buckley, that is what would have mattered most.

Women of the Bush

In the pioneering days (and for Gippsland that's not so long ago) the women had a tough time of it. Everybody knows of the heart-wrenching anxiety of the mother in Henry Lawson's epic story, 'The Drover's Wife'. And they've read George Essex Evans' poem, 'The Women of the West'. But those pieces are set in the plains country far from here. There's a story to be told about the wretched privations of some of our own womenfolk in Gippsland … and of the women who ministered to them.

Think, for instance, of the women in the mining camps at Walhalla or Stockman's Creek, or the wives of the selectors in the Strzeleckis, or the women in the timber mills out from Noojee or Erica. 'I did feel the want of a woman's society,' wrote Mrs Fuller of her husband's bush selection in 1876 near Bena. 'The men could get about better than the women – they had not the children to think of.' Such women followed their menfolk faithfully into situations that were often demeaning to themselves and detrimental to their health.

But there was another group of women to be found in the forest fastnesses and the mining camps who came by themselves, of their own volition, simply because of their calling to help these isolated women and their children. These were the churchwomen – deaconesses and medical sisters, like May Lambert or Marie Sundell or Winifred Shoobridge or Dorothy Almond, to name a few of them. They deserve to be remembered.

Mary Grant Bruce, another Gippslander, wrote about their work in an article in the West Gippsland Gazette in July, 1925:

... if your wandering should lead you to isolated hill-farms where there are no roads, and where women and children scarcely ever see a strange face; to little struggling settlements; to outback homes where life is mostly dominated by such factors as huge timber, bracken fern, and the cow, and if you should meet the women whose work, indoor and out, is never ceasing, to whom the word, "pleasure" is summed up in freedom from any acute worry, or to whom sickness or the advent of a new baby can only spell calamity – then you will find women whose eyes grow moist when they speak of the Deaconesses, and you will

hear tales of service and help that seem well-nigh incredible.

Take Winifred Shoobridge, who began her work in 1918, as our first example. She had a little Morris Oxford van to take her round the settlers' homes, but where the roads ran out and the tracks began she'd get out her bicycle from the back of her van or, more likely, borrow a horse to get further on. In Gormandale in 1922 she kept her own horse, 'Dolly'. She used Shire maps to locate and visit every family. She arranged for women in isolated places to write to one another and set up a correspondence Sunday school - the Church Mail Bag scheme – that had 2,000 members in Gippsland at one point. 'Homes can be just as much isolated by heavy timber and bad roads as those on the plains with no neighbours for 40 or 50 miles,' she wrote. Bush women would greet her with pleasure. 'Come in, you're the first woman I've seen for 10 months,' one said. 'I'm glad it's a woman who's come,' said another.

Marie Sundell offered herself from England in 1921 to come to the West Gippsland bush. Her first appointment was to Walhalla and Erica. I know one man now living in Drouin whose father was killed in an accident at a timber mill in the 1940s. This man showed me a beautiful letter written by Marie Sundell to his mother when the father was killed. The notepaper is creased and folded and the ink has faded, but it has carried its message of compassion down through eighty years and still brings tears to the eyes.

Deaconess Marie visited the outlying schools. The children at Walhalla put their money together to buy her a gift when she eventually left the district to work elsewhere. Another woman wrote of her work in Erica:

I went to Erica in 1937 ... My husband was employed in Ezard's Timber Mills. He drove a tractor [pulling a load along metal rails]*... to and from the No1 and No 2 mills, which were about ten miles out, through very rugged bush. ... The tractor was a rather crude affair with practically no shelter from the weather. But rain, hail and snow, or on the hottest day, Sister Marie would ride on it to the two mills, to do her good work. ... The trip on the tractor was really quite dangerous as the rail line, being steep in places, required sand to stop the wheels slipping. ... At one place the line was over a very high bridge and anyone else who went out with my husband would ask to be let off, but not Sister Marie. She displayed sheer doggedness ...*

The old-timers of Noojee and Fumina and Neerim South still talk about May Lambert. She's a legend up that way. She became a best friend to the women and a kindly aunty to the children in the scattered mill camps hidden away in the mountains. She was at her best during and after the terrible 1939 fires when Noojee was wiped out and many lives were lost. She actually adopted a little girl who was orphaned in the fire holocaust. Her donation of ten shillings was the first one received for the rebuilding of the little church in Noojee and her photo still hangs there today.

May Lambert also worked in and around Wonthaggi, visiting homes, caring for the sick and helping teach small children in the kindergarten. She also was instrumental in founding girl guides and boy scout troops. She wore out four Baby Austins over the years! 'Sister May always seems to bring a breath of fresh air of enthusiasm with her,' one newspaper of the day commented.

Sister Dorothy Allmond, unlike the others I've been speaking of, was a trained nurse. Dorothy worked more in East Gippsland. Her first appointment was to the Croajingalong Forest area. On one occasion, when the Bishop was visiting East Gippsland she met him on the highway and got him to come with her to help set a man's broken leg. 'I can't manage alone,' she explained. At another time, in 1924, a woman at Croajingalong was seriously ill. Eight men carried her on a stretcher in a fierce storm along sixteen miles of bush tracks to Bellbird. A newspaper of the day reported:

A feature of the task was the action of Sister Dorothy, who, when summoned, rode on horseback from Cann River to Bemm River (where the patient was), a distance of about forty miles, in about five hours. She then walked with the party giving emergency medical aid. The members of the party were exhausted after their trying ordeal in the wildest weather conditions and all were drenched with heavy rains. Their effort however was the means of saving the woman's life.

These are just four of the women who helped to bring some solace to the women and children of our pioneer settlements. I could have added the work of others – the deaconesses, Winifred Holton, Lucia Koska, Sheila Payne, Mavis Rodgers, Georgina Harvey, Sheridan Hannah, and the nursing sisters, Harriet Connley, Catherine Bennett, Ivy Gwynne, and Edith Reece. Heroines all. And, remember, they had no need to be in the parlous circumstances in which they often found themselves. They came to serve.

I leave the last word to Mary Grant Bruce:

The deaconesses have toiled with little recognition save from those with whom they actually come in contact; they ask for none. But ... it should be given them in the form in which they will value it most – that of whole-hearted sympathy, so that they may know that in every place they visited there are women who know and comprehend the greatness of their unselfish service.

Charting the Coast

The Aboriginal people lived so close to both land and sea they had no need for maps. Their maps were inside their heads. But when the first white coast-dwellers in Gippsland arrived, maps became very important. These first-comers were the sealers, many of them ex-convicts, who were dropped off from a mother ship for months at a time while they went about their business of killing seals and drying the skins. The mother ship would return in due course to pick up the men and the fruit of their labours. Maps of the coast were vital to the trade, though they were mostly rough sketches done 'on the back of an envelope'.

When the white settlement of New South Wales began in 1788, shipping along the southern coastline increased rapidly. This was the region of the roaring 'forties. Rocky headlands jagged dangerously into the sea lanes. Maps became a matter of life and death.

The names of three British sailors stand out in the exploration and charting of our Gippsland coastline – George Bass, Matthew Flinders, and John Grant.

Bass came to New South Wales as a ship's surgeon in 1795, but he was more sailor than surgeon. Almost immediately he began adventuring. He and his close friend, Flinders, began by exploring the coastline south of Sydney in a tiny vessel named the *Tom Thumb*, a twelve-foot rowing boat.

Bass was now ready for greater things. Over the New Year, December, 1797 - January, '98, with six men, he navigated an open five-oared whaleboat southward into the strait now named for him, reaching as far as Westernport. He sailed along the Ninety-Mile Beach and charted the outline of Wilson's Promontory, then called Furneaux Land, and recommended Sealers Cove as a safe harbour. Taking notice of the tides and winds, Bass reasoned it was likely that there was open water ahead and that Van Diemen's Land was therefore an island. But that remained to be proved.

It was important to find out. If a strait did indeed exist, vessels from England would be able to take the shorter route through the strait rather than make the long haul to the south of Van Diemen's Land, as all ships had done up till then, including the First Fleet. In 1798, Governor Hunter authorized an expedition to prove beyond doubt the existence of a strait separating the southern island from the mainland. The command was given to Lieutenant Matthew Flinders, who had by now established himself as an outstanding seaman and cartographer. The *Norfolk* was engaged. She had been built at the penal settlement of Norfolk Island two years earlier by convicts. This was strictly illegal - if convicts could build a boat, they could sail off in her to freedom! However the Commandant ignored orders and had the vessel built from the local Norfolk Island pine – a 23-foot single-masted sloop. She was sailed to Sydney, promptly seized by Hunter, and commissioned for Flinders' expedition.

The voyage itself, though hugely significant, was uneventful. Flinders sailed the *Norfolk* through Bass Strait, keeping to the southern shore rather than our Gippsland coast, rounded the north-west cape of Van Diemen's Land and completed the circumnavigation of the island, producing a precise chart of the entire coastline. The strait was named by Governor Hunter in honour of George Bass, while the largest island in the Strait was named Flinders Island.

Within a few years, George Bass had come to a sad end. He began trading in the Pacific. One of his ventures was a huge failure. To recoup his losses he set out in 1803 on a speculative voyage, planning to reach the west coast of South America. His ship, the *Venus*, disappeared, and was never heard of again. George Bass was thirty-two years old.

On the other hand, Flinders' greatest work - the first circumnavigation of Australia - was still to come. But not immediately. In 1800, Flinders returned to England and while there married his sweetheart, Ann Chappell. It was the beginning of a poignant love story. More in a moment! Within weeks Flinders was called back into service. Joseph Banks, the greatest naturalist of his day, convinced the British government it was vital that the whole coastline of New Holland, as it was still known, should be precisely charted. Matthew Flinders was the man to do it. He was given command of the *Investigator*, a 330-ton sloop and promoted to the rank of Commander.

Departing England in July, 1801, the *Investigator* rounded the Cape of Good Hope and sailed east across the southern Indian Ocean, sighting Cape Leeuwin in early December and began his voyage around the continent in an anticlockwise direction. Flinders sailed into Port Phillip, made an excursion to the You Yangs, climbed Arthur's Seat, and then proceeded along the Gippsland coast already familiar to him. As he sailed by, the interior of Gippsland slept peacefully in the care solely of its aboriginal inhabitants. Re-stocking in Sydney for three months, he completed the circumnavigation, passing once more through Bass Strait, reaching the end point of Sydney Harbour in June 1803. Flinders referred to the continent as 'Australia', the first person to do so.

Meanwhile Ann was waiting patiently in London for her husband's return. She waited for a further seven long years. On Flinders' return journey home, his vessel, the *Cumberland,* was forced to put in to Mauritius, French territory - and France was at war with England. Flinders was found to be carrying government papers, so was imprisoned on the island for six and a half years. It was a quite congenial imprisonment, however. Flinders had the run of the island, and had the company of his precious cat, Trim, until the latter's disappearance.

Trim had been Flinders' companion for all his voyages. Several statues of Flinders show Trim at his feet. Flinders wrote an epitaph for Trim, the words of which are inscribed on Flinders' statue outside the Mitchell Library in Sydney. Trim watches from a place nearby. The plaque reads:

TO THE MEMORY OF TRIM
The best and most illustrious of his race
The most affectionate of friends,
faithful of servants,
and best of creatures
He made the tour of the globe, and a voyage to Australia,
which he circumnavigated, and was ever the
delight and pleasure of his fellow voyagers

Eventually Flinders was released from his imprisonment and was able to join his beloved wife. Ernestine Hill has written of these things in her book, '*My Love Must Wait'*. A daughter was born, Anne, whose son, Sir William Matthew Flinders Petrie became a famous archaeologist and Egyptologist.

Sadly, Matthew Flinders did not live long. He died in London in 1814 of kidney disease. His great two-volume work, *A Voyage to Terra Australis*, arrived from the publishers the day before his death. He was aged forty.

There's a little addendum to the story. In 2019, Flinders' grave was in danger of being covered over when extension works at Euston railway station were commenced. His grave was located by archaeologists. Flinders now lies buried in more peaceful surroundings in his childhood village of Donington in Lincolnshire.

The third great name in Gippsland coastal history is that of Lieutenant James Grant. On his initial voyage to the new colony from England, Grant sailed his vessel, the *Lady Nelson*, through the newly-discovered Bass Strait in December, 1801, naming Cape Liptrap and the Glennie Islands off Wilson's Promontory, then on to his destination, Sydney.

Within a few months, Grant returned, with specific instructions from Governor King to explore and chart the southern coast. He came to Westernport and remained for some time. Grant fell in love with Westernport and in particular with Churchill Island. He had his men clear land and build a block-house. He planted out a fruit and vegetable garden with seeds given to him by an English farmer, John Churchill. Hence the name of the island. (Eight months later, Lt John Murray, who had been a member of Grant's crew, returned in the *Lady Nelson* and found a veritable harvest awaiting him, the wheat and corn six-feet high.)

Gippslanders, I've found, have a special regard for James Grant. He was the first to cultivate our soil and the first to express his love of the land. "I scarcely know a place that I should sooner call mine than this little island", he wrote of Churchill Island. Soon after, Grant sailed back to England and into obscurity, but a fitting monument to him stands at Rhyll, looking over the water to the place Grant knew and loved so well.

'One of the most significant women …'

The people of Boolarra and of Drouin and of Neerim might be surprised to learn that a woman referred to at her funeral as "one of the most significant women of the twentieth century" once lived amongst them. Her name was Joice NanKivell, better known by her married name of Joice NanKivell Loch. She has been called 'Australia's Answer to the Scarlet Pimpernel' and 'Mother Teresa with a dash of Indiana Jones'. There's a good deal of information about her available, but in telling her story I'm relying mostly on a book by Susanna de Vries, "Blue Ribbons, Bitter Bread', that I picked up in an Op Shop in Wonthaggi.

Joice was born into luxury on a Queensland sugar farm, but the abolition of kanaka labour and the onset of the 1890s Depression combined to ruin that way of life and the family came to a run-down Boolarra farm when Joice was a young girl. They travelled to Morwell by train, then a half-day journey by buggy took them through dense and dripping gums over rutted bush tracks to their new home. De Vries describes the place:

Behind the paling stockade, built to keep out the livestock,
they saw a small wooden shack with dirt-encrusted
windows. Two slab sheds – the kitchen and toilet – sagged
against the wooden walls of the shack ... It consisted of
three small dark rooms, lined with stained newspapers and
hessian sugar bags to block out the biting wind which
whistled through the weatherboards. ... The kitchen was an
ancient shed without any water supply. It had a dirt floor,
one small cupboard, a wobbly pine table and half an
upended kerosene tin to serve as a sink.

It was a miserable existence for them all, made worse by the inadequacies of Joice's shiftless father. We don't often hear of this side of rural life in those times before the First World War. The accounts we do hear tend to come from those who made a success of their farming ventures. For instance, the classic text on rural life in the Strzeleckis in that era – *Land of the Lyrebird* – was written by 'the winners', those who won through over their hardships. But many didn't. The NanKivell family at Boolarra was amongst them.

After failing at Boolarra they moved to a property at Myrrhee in north-east Victoria, then, after a short spell in Melbourne, returned to Gippsland. Their new place was south of Drouin, probably at Lardner, keeping livestock and growing vegetables and fruit, notably cherries Things were not much better here. Joice at age fourteen was the oldest pupil in the school and acted as a monitor, helping with school organisation and with the smaller pupils' classes. Beyond that, she worked on the farm for over ten years without pay or pocket-money. As Joice matured into an attractive and intelligent young woman, her world revolved around her reading and her care for the animals on the farm. The medical knowledge she gained later came to be very useful to her.

Joice had a world vision that the narrow confines of life on the farm and the hard rural surroundings of West Gippsland failed to satisfy. As a sign of this, she wrote a children's book echoing the longings of herself and her younger brother, *The Cobweb Ladder*, in which two children climb a cobweb ladder and discover a make-believe magic world. Occasionally Joice had a break from the drudgery of hard farm labour. With her mother, she travelled to Lakes Entrance for holidays and surfed on the Ninety-Mile Beach.

From Drouin, Joice and her parents moved to a forty-acre farm at Neerim. Here, life was a little easier for the family.

Joice published some poetry and prepared her children's book for publication. With the outbreak of war in 1914, Joice, then twenty-seven, left her parents at Neerim and moved to Melbourne. The War brought tragedy as well as change. Joice's brother, Geoff, went off to Gallipoli and then to the Western Front. His death in action was devastating for Joice. She found consolation in her poetry and preparing her next book, *The Solitary Pedestrian*, a series of sketches about her growing up.

Joice began working as a research assistant to the Warden of Trinity College in the University of Melbourne and was able to attend lectures. Her literary work developed. She published more of her poems and joined the Lyceum Club, a Society for women engaged in the arts. Joice also began to review books for the Melbourne *Herald*. It was through this that she met her husband, Sydney Loch. Loch had fought at Gallipoli and been invalided home. He wrote a book about his experiences, *The Straits Impregnable*, which gave such a vivid picture of Gallipoli that it was banned by the censor because of the negative effect it might have on public morale. However, Joice reviewed the book in her *Herald* column, which led to their meeting and then their marriage and extraordinary life together over the next thirty-five years.

With the war over, Joice and Sydney travelled to England and began, jointly, to investigate and involve themselves in various trouble spots in Europe. They went to Ireland during the Troubles and published a book, *Ireland in Travail*. They went on to eastern Poland and worked with the Quakers amongst the thousands of peasants who had been thrown off their land through Russian incursions. Joice's incredible hands-on work led to an award by the Polish government. Joice and Sydney's book, *The River of a Hundred Ways* told the story of the emergency there and of the relief effort they were part of. Joice's humanitarian instincts were by now the driving force of her life and she spent the next fifty years, until her death in 1982, working amongst displaced and refugee people in Europe, particularly in Poland and in Greece.

In the 'twenties, the Lochs moved to Salonica (Thessaloniki) in Greece to assist Greek refugees who had been forced out of Turkey. Joice worked as a nurse – virtually as a doctor - and organised work and education for the refugees. Her work was nothing short of heroic. From there the Lochs moved to Ouranoupolis near Mount Athos where Joice again worked, unsparing of herself, amongst the refugee population. She established a rug – making industry to provide work for the poverty-ridden people there. Ouranoupolis remained Joice's base for the rest of her life.

Still more vital work lay ahead. In 1939, the Nazis occupied Poland. Polish refugees – Jews and others - poured into Rumania. Sure enough, Joice and Sydney were there in Bucharest working once more with the Friends' Relief Service to provide aid. In perhaps the most dramatic and heroic episode of her life, Joice gathered some hundreds of the most vulnerable refugees together – women and children - and took them by train and steamer to Istanbul and then by ship to safety in Cyprus, sailing through heavily-mined seas, and then on to Haifa in Palestine. Joice and Sydney spent the rest of the War in Palestine assisting with humanitarian work amongst refugees from both Turkey and Greece.

After the War the Lochs returned to Ouranoupolis. Sydney died in 1955, but Joice remained there for a further thirty years, devoting herself to the local people. Their rugs brought high prices in the United States, Britain, and

Australia. Joice continued to write. The income from her books paid for a water-supply for the village.

Joice NanKivell Loch was honoured throughout Europe and especially in Greece. She received rewards and honours from the governments of Greece, Rumania, and Poland and Britain. No Australian woman has been more widely honoured, not even Nancy Wake, the 'White Mouse' of the Second World War, who is much better known to the general public. Sadly, however, most Australians know nothing of her. The only recognition of the family in Gippsland that I know of is that her brother, Geoff, has his name inscribed on the War Memorial at the entrance to the Neerim Cemetery.

Bushrangers great and small

We don't generally associate Gippsland with bushrangers, although there are numerous episodes of armed robberies in the Gippsland bush, and Gippsland was at least touched by the activities of some of the more 'celebrated' men of the road. 'Mad' Dan Morgan, for instance, worked at George Black's Tarwin West run before he took to the road. And there seems little doubt that Ned Kelly used the fastnesses of the Gippsland high country during his reign of terror. Edward Bennett of Stratford knew him. He was 'a decent young man,' according to Bennett. 'I always felt sorry he ever went bushranging.'

Many of the bushrangers, like Ned Kelly, turned to the game because of some trivial episode where they were treated unfairly by those in authority. Others acted on the spur of the moment. Such a one was George de Thouars, who, in 1877 was working at Edward Crooke's *Holey Plain* near Rosedale. His was a particularly inept crime. Momentarily angered by a slight, he bailed up the household and workers before riding off on one of the station's horses. He quickly repented and handed himself in. Despite his contrition he was sentenced to fifteen years hard labour. This was at the time when the Kellys were still at large, and it seems without doubt that de Thouars' sentence reflected community feeling against them rather than fitting his own case. Despite a huge campaign for a remission of sentence, he served more than seven years before the Governor saw fit to remit the remainder of his sentence.

Other bushranging episodes result from a twisted mind. The newspapers of the day treated the case of Conrad Ballantyne and the Fumina shootings in 1921 without much humanity. Annie O'Reilly, in her excellent 'Odd Australian History' online series is much more sympathetic. Fumina is a small settlement under the shadow of Mount Baw Baw. Everyone knows everyone else. Young Conrad Ballantyne took a gun that belonged to one of his friends and, with neither rhyme nor reason, shot and wounded the post-mistress and her step-daughter. At his trial he was deemed to be insane and was committed to a lunatic asylum where he died a few years later. It seems likely that the lad's mind was turned by a mind-shattering experience earlier in his life when he was lost in the bush for two weeks during extremely harsh winter conditions.

However, the saddest case of local 'bushranging' occurred in the Neerim district the next year, 1922. I was alerted to the centenary of this matter by a snippet in the *Warragul and Drouin Gazette* which runs a series on events of 100 years ago. In late March, 1922, a local boy, Henry Maple, and his mate, Robert Banks, broke into a Neerim Junction store and stole a tent, a pea-rifle, ammunition, and other goods. It was the beginning of a week-long saga that ended with the death of Maple and the capture of Banks. Maple was fifteen, Banks, eighteen.

A sociologist could easily see the pattern that lay behind these tragic events. Both boys had spent time in a reformatory because they could not be managed at home. Maple was tall, heavy, rangy, ungainly. He preferred the company of older boys and men. He had adopted the ways of older men, in particular heavy smoking. He hated to be confined and lived for the open air and the bush. He knew all about the exploits of the Kellys and the bushrangers of forty or fifty years earlier. He had an obsession with guns and had become a crack shot. Banks claimed that Maple could hit a sixpence thrown in the air at fifty yards. How often we hear about an interest in firearms becoming an obsession and leading to criminal acts.

The week of terror, as the press labelled it, began on Sunday night, 19 March. Banks was staying at the Maple farm near Neerim Junction. During the night they took off, broke into the store, and took to the bush, their intention, apparently, being to work their way to Melbourne. Maple was the controlling partner. In the best tradition of bushranging (*"'I'll fight but not surrender", said the wild Colonial boy'*!), he told Banks that he would die rather than be taken. Local men began to search for them. In one foray, the two were separated and a returned soldier, George Woolstencroft, captured Banks, who was carrying a shot-gun, leaving Maple with the pea-rifle. Woolstencroft returned to the search area and was shot by Maple, a bullet penetrating his lung. He was driven to the hospital in Warragul, were he eventually made a full recovery.

The nation's press was now fully engaged. Banner headlines carried the latest news. Pen-pictures of Neerim Junction spoke of crowds milling outside the store. The affair was the 'Neerim Sensation'. The couple were referred to as the 'boy bushrangers'. Maple was labelled 'a young desperado'. The searchers were told to 'shoot on sight', the papers declared.

On Monday, 27 March, the end came. News was instantly telegraphed through to the 'Sun':

Armed pursuers came upon Henry Maple, the second boy bushranger, in the dense scrub about a mile from Neerim today, and, taking no chances, they shot him between the eyes. The boy fell, dangerously wounded.

The final stand was at Glen Nayook, now a peaceful gully, with tall tree-ferns standing by a clear stream, lyrebirds calling from the timber on either side. Maple took his last stand behind a huge fallen tree. As a dozen men surrounded him – police and volunteers, all armed with .303 rifles – the lad stood and fired at them. A volley of fire was returned, supposed to be aimed over his head, but as the boy fell and the men rushed forward, they found a bullet had entered his forehead and lodged in his brain. He died soon after arriving at Warragul hospital. Some believed he may have committed suicide, but Dr Trumpy's evidence at the inquest pointed otherwise.

Some people had kind words to say to the family. Maple's former teacher wrote a sympathetic letter. The papers were less forgiving. The Melbourne Herald, even on the day of the boy's death, railed:

Bushranging has an overpowering fascination for some natures, as the case of Henry Maple of Neerim proves. The call to such, apparently, is irresistible, although its history in Australia tells mainly of sordid and murderous deeds wrought upon unarmed people and privation and hardship ending inevitably in degradation or disgraceful death for the bushranger. Brought up in the bush, and instinct with the desire for woodcraft and skill with arms, the murderous youth who is now hunted down could have seen only the glamor of the life and sought its excitements with all the vanity of an ill-regulated mind.

Henry Maple has been lying in the Neerim cemetery now for a hundred years. He looks down to Glen Nayook where he met his end and across to where his family once farmed. Magpies salute the rising sun and farewell the day at its end. Time has passed … and perhaps we would have kinder words to say about Henry now than in the harsher days of yesteryear. At least there was some respect shown for him at the time: amongst those who carried his coffin were some who had sought him with loaded rifles a few days earlier.

Winners of the Melbourne Cup

It was the first Tuesday in November, 1946, mid-afternoon, and Mr Barker disappeared from our Maths class. I was in Form 3 at Warragul High School. He returned a few minutes later. 'Who won?' we asked. 'Joseph Stalin,' he muttered. We knew immediately. 'Russia', of course - by five lengths, at 16 to 1, it turned out.

The Melbourne Cup has been the Holy Grail of Australian racing for 160 years. Twice, the Cup has come to Gippsland. I'm discounting Colonus's win. *Colonus* won in the mud in 1942. His owner was Lou Menck who had a property at Labertouche and Colonus used to spell on the place. But Menck didn't live there, so I don't count that as a truly Gippsland cup. And I give my condolences, in passing, to the Hon William Pearson of Kilmany Park, Rosedale, who went very close. His horse, Commotion, ran third in 1883, and the next year, his two entries, Commotion and Plausible, ran second and third. There's sometimes a thin line between glory and inconsequence!

The first genuine Gippsland cup winner was Wollomai in 1875. As you might guess, the horse came from Phillip

Island. A bay horse, 6 y o, entire. He was owned by Captain John Cleeland from Cape Woolamai (note the different spelling). Born in County Down in 1928, Cleeland joined the Californian gold rush in the early 1850s, then bought the schooner, *Harriet*, which traded out of San Francisco around the Pacific. Cleeland became a fervent supporter of the Confederate cause in the American Civil War. He named one of his racehorses, Shenandoah, after the celebrated Confederate warship that visited Melbourne while the Civil War was still in active contention. In Melbourne, Cleeland ran a leading Bourke Street Hotel, the Albion (where the Cobb & Co coaches set off for Gippsland and elsewhere) and bought 7000 acres at Cape Woolamai where he built a substantial home, Woolamai House, at Newhaven. For some reason I can't discover, he used the pseudonym, H Sharp, as the owner of his horse, Wollomai.

1875 was the first year the Melbourne Cup had been held on a Tuesday, but any doubts about the change of date were dispelled when 70,000 turned up to see the race – about one-tenth of Melbourne's population. The smart money was on Imperial which was sent out favourite at 3/1. Wollomai had too much condition, it was claimed, but he

103

nevertheless had some support and started at 16/1. He'd won the Warrnambool Cup over the same distance, two miles. Besides, Bob Batty was aboard – the great Bob Batty, equally good on the flat as over fences. Batty knew he was on a good thing. He held his horse back in the early stages, but he was challenging at the half-mile, took the lead in the strait and got his mount home comfortably by two lengths. "The grey and gold jacket of Mr Cleeland's horse passed the post the easiest of winners", the Herald reported. Cleeland went home with the £1,265 first prize and, characteristically, gave Steve Moon, the trainer, and Batty £500 each. He could afford his liberality, however. It was rumoured that he had won over £20, 000 from the bookmakers. Later, he retained Batty as his full-time trainer

There's a little more to be said, however. Wollomai travelled to the course on foot. That involved swimming the Narrows to get from the Island to San Remo, then walking the eighty miles (130 kilometres) to the course over several days during the week before the race. Perhaps he lost some of that condition! It's said around the Island that some of Cleeland's horses were stolen by members of the Kelly Gang and used in their escapades Not Wollomai himself, however! Captain John Cleeland lived on at

Woolamai House until he died in 1914. As an old sea-captain, he used to sit in his chair by a window, looking out over the water, keeping a spyglass handy to check on the weather and passing ships in the night.

After forty years in the wilderness, the Melbourne Cup again came to Gippsland. Patrobas won the Cup in 1915. Mrs Edith Widdis, nee Nixon, was the owner. The Widdises and the Nixons are old Gippsland names. John Widdis's family began by carting and milling timber, using bullock teams. By 1915, the family fortunes had progressed to the point that John and Edith held a huge Nambrok property, ensconced in a magnificent mansion, Nambrok House, with a sprawl of buildings around the house, including the stables where their racehorses were housed. They're there to this day. Both John and Edith were keen patrons of the turf and competed in good humour with each other as to whose horses would win the most races.

In November 1915 the First World War had been in progress for over a year. Australian forces had been in operation on the Gallipoli Peninsula for many months. Many questioned whether sports fixtures, including racing, should continue. Racing survived, largely because the Racing Clubs offered to donate all profits to the war effort.

105

Amongst the 90,000 at Flemington on Cup Day, 1915, were many wounded AIF returnees, as well as many others in service uniforms. On the opening day of the Cup carnival, Edith Widdis's brown 3 yo colt, Patrobas, ridden by W Smart, won the Derby in scintillating fashion. Patrobas, a grandson of the famous Carbine, had been bought as a 2 y o the previous year for 300 guineas. In the Cup a few days later, Smart was replaced by Bobby Lewis. Smart couldn't make the light weight Patrobas was to carry (7lb 6 oz). However Bobby Lewis was the finest rider of his day. Lewis, riding 'long', standing tall in the saddle, was said to be 'soft' with his mounts, riding with hands and heels rather than with the whip.

A huge field of thirty-six horses lined up at the barrier, and it took a long time for the starter to settle the line into order. Soon after the start, three horses came down. Lewis skilfully avoided the fallen horses, got his horse back to the rails and stayed there until the home turn. Faced with a wall of horse, Lewis took Patrobas four-wide on the turn. In the dash to the post, Patrobas put his nose in front with fifty yards to go and got home by half a length.

The victory was the first Cup win ever achieved by a horse raced by a woman. Special permission had to be given for

Mrs Widdis to enter the hallowed halls of the Victoria Racing Club, where women were excluded. The rules were bent; Mrs Widdis attended the traditional Cup reception at the Club and placated the critics by donating the cost of the reception to the war effort.

The bookmakers paid out at 8 to 1 on the winner. It was not only the Widdises, but many Gippslanders who had a smile on their face and a large cheque in their pocket as a result of Patrobas' win. John Widdis had the chance to win back the honours from his wife the following year when his horse, Shepherd King, ran in the Cup, but the horse was beaten into second place.

Sadly, some ill-feeling developed subsequent to Patrobas's Cup win. The trainer, Charlie Wheeler, felt he had been hard done by in the matter of his reward. Mrs Widdis had given him £500 as a gift. Wheeler believed he was entitled to 10% of the winning stake, which amounted to a higher figure and brought an action against Mrs Widdis. The judge, however found in favour of the defendant, though awarded costs against her.

Ninety years after Patrobas's famous victory, the citizens of Rosedale, on the Highway just a short distance from

Nambrok House, decided to put up a statue of Patrobas. You may see him there today as you drive past – Patrobas, at full gallop, Bobby Lewis's eyes fixed on the winning post ahead.

The Medicine Men

Nearly all country towns remember a particular doctor who worked tirelessly over a long time, performing amazing feats of medicine. The people of old Yallourn speak lovingly of Dr James Andrew. In Orbost, Dr James Kerr, the first doctor ever to come to the town, served the people devotedly for four decades. In Bunyip, Dr Dick Baldwin is remembered for his cricket as well as his doctoring, and died on the cricket field. In Warragul, two doctor father-and-sons, David and Oswald Trumpy and George and Conrad Ley, cared for the welfare of the town over fifty years. In naming these men, I acknowledge that they are representative of a wider group of loyal medical practitioners throughout Gippsland who performed miracles of healing, often under extremely difficult conditions.

By 1889, Orbost was becoming a settled community, although still a scattered grouping of rudimentary buildings surrounded by scrub. Surprisingly, there was a Branch of the Friendly Society, MUIOOF, in town. They began a search for a doctor and eventually arranged to sponsor

James Kerr from Scotland. He arrived in that year, 1889. He must have been shocked by the severe rural conditions that awaited him. Nevertheless, he threw himself into his work for the local community. He married a local girl, Hilda Temple, the poet, daughter of the local storekeeper. His practice was virtually limitless. He travelled far and wide on horseback to answer calls for his help. In one dreadful case, in 1900, Dr Kerr was called to Marlo and on to Cape Conran, to treat the victims of a shocking fire tragedy where three children were burnt to death and other members of the family severely injured. James Kerr died in 1928, aged sixty-five, and is commemorated in Orbost by a set of stained glass windows in St James' Church dedicated to *Dr James Kerr, Beloved Physician of Orbost'*. Also, the Infant Welfare Centre is named in honour of him.

James Andrew came to Yallourn in December, 1925, shortly after its establishment by the State Electricity Commission as 'an ideal town'. When he died in 1972, he had become 'the Father of Yallourn'. He is remembered as much for his civic involvement as his medical work. As a doctor he was deeply respected for his surgical and general expertise. After all, he had topped the medical course at

Melbourne University alongside his good friend and walking companion, McFarlane Burnet. His ability to understand and sympathise with the people of Yallourn came, I think, from his own rural beginnings at Colbinabbin, near Rochester. Andrew threw himself into local organisations like the Scouts, the Orchestral Society, the Presbyterian Church (St Andrew's!), the Golf Club, and the eisteddfod. He was a man of boundless energy and enthusiasm. His T-model Ford was a talking point of the town, especially when it refused to start! In civic affairs, he was the town's spokesperson on many occasions As a leading member of the Yallourn Civic Association, he stood up to the authority of the State Electricity Commission in such matters as making the town's news-sheet, 'Livewire' a reflection of the community rather than a mouthpiece for the Commission or, in another matter, turning the Commission's general store into a co-operative, owned by the community.

Dr Andrew worked through the building of the Yallourn Hospital and became Yallourn's Chief Medical Officer. He did his best to overcome the unhealthy effects of the coal-dust that infiltrated everything, including people's lungs. He believed Yallourn should have been built where Brown

111

Coal Mine (now Yallourn North) is, above the fog and dust of Yallourn. No doctor has been better memorialized than James Andrew. Old Gippstown at Moe has taken a former Yallourn house and filled it with Dr Andrew's personal possessions. You can see there his desk, just as he might have stood up from it, his chair, his books, his camera, his photographs, his diaries, his camping and golf gear, his sketch book, his beetle collection, even his doctor's bag.

Early Warragul was fortunate in having several doctors of strong repute and long standing. When Dr David Trumpy arrived in Warragul from Drouin in 1888, he took over the practice of Dr John Cobb in Victoria Street. John Cobb had been in Warragul since the earliest days of the town. Years later he was remembered as 'one pioneer who should not be forgotten ... whose kindness to his poorer patients could never be paid for with money'. Indeed, the people of Warragul, as throughout West Gippsland, had very little to spare. It was not uncommon for the doctor's fee to be paid for in kind, such as a pound of butter or a fat chook. Dr Cobb ended his time in Warragul on a poignant note. When typhoid broke out in the town, he pulled each of the victims through, but his own daughter, nineteen years old, he could not save. I believe this personal tragedy was the reason he gave up his work.

David Trumpy was born in Switzerland and studied medicine in both Switzerland and Italy. Throughout his time in Warragul he kept up with the Swiss community in Melbourne and made several trips back to his native land. In Warragul, his house served as a kind of hospital, perhaps more like a sick-bay. *'Persons desiring to obtain better attention and comfort than they can get at their own homes, can be accommodated at Dr Trumpy's house, Terms on application',* he advertised soon after his arrival. As the Shire's Medical Officer, he constantly campaigned to have the gutters formed and open cess-pools covered. Typhoid remained a risk for many years. Horse manure would constantly clog the drains and provide a source of infection.

It was Dr Trumpy's practice to ride rather than use a jinker. Once, when riding to visit a patient along the Brandy Creek Road, he was thrown off his horse. While he was convalescing, Dr Hayes saw to his practice. (Dr Hayes was another pioneering doctor in Warragul who deserves recognition). Dr Trumpy and his wife ran their private hospital, Cooinda', at 63 Victoria Street until their retirement in 1925.

113

In 1911, after twenty-three years in Warragul, Dr Trumpy and his wife left for a thirteen-month trip to Europe, spent mostly in Switzerland and Italy. At a testimonial dinner at the Railway Hotel before his departure, the Mayor, Count von Horn, presided and presented Dr Trumpy with a silver writing case. The local paper reported:

The loyal toast was honored and then the toast of "Our guest" elicited numerous speeches which clearly indicated the high esteem and affection felt for Dr Trumpy by all classes throughout the district.

In many surgical cases, Dr Trumpy worked with Dr George Ley. Often, Dr Ley performed the operation while Dr Trumpy administered the chloroform. The two worked in tandem for many years. The first Warragul Hospital was built during this time on a three-acre parcel of land donated by Mrs Mary Sergeant. Dr Ley was particularly active in the establishment of the hospital and its development over many years until his death.

These two foundational Warragul doctors, David Trumpy and George Ley, are commemorated by the naming of Trumpy Lane near the town centre and Ley Street alongside the hospital. Both left sons to carry on their work – Dr Oswald Trumpy and Dr Conrad Ley*.

Throughout Gippsland, men and women of the medical profession have always evoked a warm feeling of respect from the community. That respect began with the selfless service of men like James Kerr, James Andrew, David Trumpy, George Ley, and many others who went beyond the call of duty in the turbulent early days of settlement.

*Both Oswald Trumpy and Conrad Ley have football connections. Oswald Trumpy was President of the Warragul Football Club at the time of his untimely death in 1945. A few years later, in 1952, Conrad Ley, then a surgeon at Prince Henry's Hospital, saved the life of star Carlton forward, Keith Warburton, after an onfield internal injury, and was rewarded with Life Membership of the Club.

The Haunted Stream

In Gippsland, the gold fields were mostly in rugged bushland country. The men who tried their luck in these places were often young, single, and hot-blooded. Disputes, often fuelled by grog, sometimes led to violence and in some cases murder. However the two separate murders committed at the Haunted Stream in the second half of the nineteenth century were deeds of cold-blooded calculation.

The Omeo diggings opened up in 1853. A series of rushes in nearby streams followed. In 1857, the rush at the Haunted Stream (yet to receive its name) was in full swing and the usual motley collection of men had gathered, living and working and scheming their lives away. One of these was a very distinctive man known to everybody as Ballarat Harry. He was well-spoken, well-educated, and was reckoned to carry quite a deal of cash on his person. Later, when the Tichborne Case erupted, it was widely held that Ballarat Harry was in fact the missing heir to the Tichborne fortune, Sir Roger Tichborne. This is the reason the case of Ballarat Harry received so much publicity.

On the diggings there weren't many secrets. Everyone knew everyone else and all their doings. One of Ballarat Harry's workmates was a man called Thomas Toke. Toke was something of a mystery man himself, and a man of letters, too, judging by a letter from him I've come across, full of high-blown phrases and quoting Shakespeare into the bargain. Toke and Ballarat Harry went off to search for a new El Dorado said to exist in the vicinity. A week later Toke returned alone, apparently with some of Ballarat Harry's possessions, including his horse, some of his gold, and also a large amount of cash. Ballarat Harry was never seen again, and Toke was charged with his murder.

There are many variations of what eventuated on that infamous trip. Between the many contradictory accounts that were given out over succeeding years, I've wound my way to what I believe to be the facts of the matter. First of all, Ballarat Harry's name was actually Harry Clare, and he was not Sir Roger Tichborne! Toke and Harry went together to Omeo. Toke's story was that on the trip he bought Harry's horse legitimately and won some of his possessions through gambling. The two men also exchanged some of their gold nuggets. They proceeded into the open country further to the west, where they parted,

Harry declaring that he might go on to Adelaide or to Boggy Creek. At the trial, several witnesses backed up the defendant by stating that Toke previously had large amounts of money. Without a body and without certain proof, the charge of murder was dismissed, although Toke was given a seven year sentence for horse-stealing.

Shortly after this, matters that were covered up at Toke's trial were brought to light in an unexpected way. A gold buyer, Cornelius Green, was murdered near Omeo in a particularly callous killing. Two men were charged and convicted of the crime and subsequently hanged. One of them, William Armstrong, while awaiting execution, voluntarily provided information about Harry Clare's murder. He stated that Thomas Toke had put it to him that they should together kill Ballarat Harry and get off with his money. Armstrong refused to be in it, upon which Toke told him that if he didn't 'split' he would give him £100. When Toke eventually returned alone from his exploration, they both kept their bargain. Armstrong didn't 'split' and Toke paid over the £100. No further action was taken. Toke lived out his life a free man. Nearly thirty years later the part-remains of a man's body were found in the bush near Omeo. The skull was crushed and it was widely believed that the remains were those of Harry Clare. But like so much in this matter, the truth was never firmly established, enabling the story of 'Ballarat Harry' to remain a matter of conjecture and mystery. Harry's ghost was said to have returned to the diggings to haunt his killer. The creek was given the name, the 'Haunted Stream' and it is marked on maps to this day.

By 1892 the first flush of alluvial gold in the Haunted Stream had passed and had given way to deep-lead reef mining. The small town of Stirling had come into existence and was now in decline. Fewer than twenty people lived there. A handful of scattered huts and shacks, some empty, clung together around the store. The store is central to our story. John Cohen was the shopkeeper for several years until he handed it on to David Tait for two years while he was in Melbourne running a produce business near the Sarah Sands Hotel in Brunswick. He then returned to Stirling and joined Tait in ownership of the store. He was thirty-four years old, and single. The arrangement was that Tait worked his claim while Cohen looked after the business. They shared a one-roomed timber and corrugated-iron hut some twenty metres from the store itself. The hut was built off the ground, standing on wooden piers. The night of 6 August, 1892 seemed normal enough. The store was locked up. Tait and Cohen were asleep in their bunks nearby. In the early hours, at about one o'clock (the time varies with each report), the stillness of the little settlement was rocked by a huge explosion. Cohen's brother lived in a shack fifty metres away. He ran to find his brother's hut completely demolished. Tait lay under a pile of rubble, not seriously injured. His brother's dismembered body lay some ten metres away, apparently blown clear through the roof.

The facts of the crime were quickly put together. Two and a half kilograms of dynamite had been stolen from a shed at the back of the store. A length of fuse wire had been stolen previously from the store itself. The perpetrator had placed the dynamite under the hut in which the two men slept, purposefully or accidentally directly beneath Cohen's bed. A seven-metre fuse led from the explosive to the adjoining laneway. The fuse had been lit there and would have taken seven and a half minutes to burn to the explosive device – plenty of time to make good an escape.

The investigating police reasoned that the act was one of accident, suicide (with or without an accomplice), or murder. The first two possibilities were quickly ruled out.

All possible suspects were investigated. The newspapers across the nation trumpeted the details of this 'dastardly and premeditated outrage'. They hinted at likely suspects. Cohen was of quiet and sober habits. He had no enemies. There were no strangers in the vicinity. Cohen's brother offered a £50 reward and the government matched it. The residents of the tiny settlement lived in uneasy suspicion of one of their number being a cold-blooded murderer.

Time passed. The trail gradually ran cold. The police investigator was transferred elsewhere. The newspapers splashed ink over the matter every now and then, but gradually the matter passed into the realm of one of the great unsolved mysteries of the mountains.

The Haunted Stream now quietly runs its course down to the Tambo and on into the Lakes and then to the great southern sea. Only the ghosts know the truth of the dark secrets of its past.

The Grand Ridge Road

The early settlers of Gippsland found it difficult to get through the westernmost parts of the region. As well as the dense forests, the terrain was steep in most places, and where the mountains or the forests ended, the swamps began. However some trails developed. They grew with little planning, following the tracks made in the earliest times. There were three such east-west tracks – Old Sale Road and Old Telegraph Road in the centre and McDonald's Track to the south. However another road was developed which was more artificial. It was a product of perceived need. This was the Grand Ridge Road.

The Grand Ridge Road runs roughly along the crest of the Strzelecki Mountains. Selectors in the late nineteenth century opened up the western end of the Strzeleckis, despite huge difficulties. The forest was eventually overcome and productive farms came into existence. Towns like Poowong, Leongatha, and Korumburra were established. Further east, however, far from sources of supply and dealing with poorer and steeper country, the settlers largely failed. Much of the bush was part-cleared and then abandoned. When the First World War broke out, young men left to enlist and seldom returned after the war had ended. Exhausted settlers walked away from their farms. By the 1920s, blackberries, rabbits, and bracken had taken over.

Still, some clung to the belief that these eastern parts of the Strzeleckis could be redeemed. The saving element was to be a new road that would link the isolated pockets, replacing the poorly-constructed, muddy dirt tracks and roads then existing. Besides, it was argued, the new road would be a scenic wonder. Tourism would be a key to rejuvenating the area.

Until 1913 Victorian roads were under the control of local authorities. In the Strzeleckis a hotchpotch of roads developed, each serving a local need but not linked into a master-plan. In 1913 the Country Roads Board was established to co-ordinate development of our road system. Its initial investigations into the State's roads were delayed by the First War, but by 1925 a grand plan was produced. Part of this plan was the building of a road to link the isolated and decaying Strzelecki hill towns. Interestingly, the road fell under the Board's 'Isolated Settlers Roads' portfolio. The road became known, in 1933, as the Grand Ridge Road.

The scheme was unsuccessful. The hoped-for resurgence in hill-country development failed to occur. The road was a scenic wonder, certainly, but a white elephant economically. The situation was well summed up by an acute and imaginative observer, T J Hogan, in the 'Argus' in 1935:

The Grand Ridge Road lies across the tragic splendour of South Gippsland like a long ruffle cast before a prankish wind. Up and down, in and out, clinging to the brims of tall hills precariously, winding above the depths of gullies and gorges, where giant mountain ashes leap skyward through tree-fern and blackwood; running along the tops of ridges with views that seem to reach to the borders of eternity. ... There is a divine madness lurking in the Australian bush, even where the hand of man has desecrated and cast aside the beauty that would have transformed him. ... Then, past Gunyah and Boolarra, is the land of the great black stumps and the kindly bracken which tries to hold what man has abandoned: narrow valleys and wind-swept pastures, decaying fences, and squalid, often tenantless homes that the merciful green would hide. ... Much of this district bears sad testimony to an enthusiastic rather than reasonable attempt to populate the land under a scheme of closer settlement without adequate consideration of the peculiarities of the country.

Today the scars of yesterday are largely hidden by fresh re-growth of timber. Hobby farms here and there bring a semblance of occupation. However, business acumen will always seek to fill a vacuum, and here it is the softwood industry that has come in to turn the land into greater productivity. Plantations of softwood (mostly radiata pine) and hardwood (mostly blue gum) cover broad acres of land in the eastern Strzeleckis. A huge pine nursery at Gelliondale, near Alberton, supplies the seedlings. The turning over of land to single-use purpose is highly debatable. Environmental issues, such as vegetation bio-diversity, species survival (the koala, for one), and risks of wildfire still hang in the balance.

Away from the plantation forests, however, the natural landscape exists in many delightful pockets. The Mount Worth State Park at the western end of the Road has over 1000 hectares of original mountain ash and attractive forest re-growth. Although this is a State Park, it came about through local efforts, namely by the Warragul Field

125

Naturalists Club and the former Shire of Warragul. The Friends of Mount Worth help to keep the Park in good trim.

Further east along the Grand Ridge Road is the Tarra-Bulga National Park. (There is little difference between a State Park and a National Park. National Parks are usually larger and contain more diverse and unspoilt landscapes. In Victoria, both have been managed by the Department of Environment, Land, Water and Planning.) Whereas the Mount Worth State Park looks out to the north, Tarra-Bulga seems to belong more to the south. The original impetus came when the Shire of Alberton in 1903 persuaded the State government to set aside twenty hectares of fern gullies near Balook as a public park. It was named 'Bulga', an aboriginal word for 'mountain'. In 1909 the State set aside 300 hectares in the nearby Tarra Valley. This was named 'Tarra' after the Tarra River and ultimately after Charlie Tarra, the aboriginal man who guided Count Paul Strzelecki through the forests and scrub south from here on his journey of exploration in 1840, and who virtually saved the whole party from dying of exposure and starvation. In 1986, an exchange of land was arranged with APM Forests. This enabled the two Parks to be combined under the present name of Tarra-Bulga National Park. The current size of the Park is 2015 hectares. Since 2018 the Park has come under the control of Parks Victoria, a Statutory Authority of the Victorian government. There are superb walking trails in the Tarra-Bulga National Park. If you want to recapture in some measure what vast parts of Gippsland were like before the intervention of the white 'invaders' you can do that here better than any anywhere else and on a wider scale. Parks Victoria consults carefully with the people from the Brataualung tribe whose ancestors trod these paths millennia ago.

As I drive now along the Grand Ridge Road, I'm reminded of another vehicle that travelled this road in February, 1977. The driver was Ronald James Eastwood, a prison escapee, and in the back of the vehicle were the nine children from the Wooreen School and their teacher, Robert Hunter, chained together. Wooreen is in the Strzelecki hills north from Leongatha and west from Mirboo North. Eastwood had kidnapped the whole school, bundled them into the van, pinned a note on the school door to tell the parents the children were on a bush walk, and headed east along the Grand Ridge Road. At Mirboo North he stopped at the Post Office and posted a ransom demand to the Minister for Education. Continuing, Eastwood crashed the van into a timber truck and took further hostages until eventually one of them escaped and the whole plot uncoiled. Eastwood went back to prison for a long time.

The road is still the same as it was then - gravel surface in long stretches, twisty, narrow, and hilly. Timber trucks still await around the next bend. A scenic delight, with views that seem to reach 'to the borders of eternity' … but you need to keep your eyes on the road ahead!

Land of the Lyrebird

In March, 1913, some of the pioneer settlers of the South Gippsland forests gathered for a reunion. Someone suggested they should write their memoirs before memories of the early days were forgotten. The result was the book, *Land of the Lyrebird*, which was eventually published in 1920. Of the seventy separate pieces in the book, only six were written by women. I've taken one of those articles to represent all the others, and I've chosen one of the women writers because I believe that, generally speaking, they suffered more from their difficulties than did the men. I'll let Mrs W J Williams tell her own story.

About the second of June, 1886, I bade farewell to my parents and friends in the Ballarat district, and started on the first stage of my journey to South Gippsland, where my husband had preceded me. My first baby was then seven weeks' old. I travelled to Melbourne with Miss Rainbow, who was going to Gippsland also. We stayed in Melbourne that night, and went as far as Drouin the next day [by train], staying the night there. The following morning we started for Poowong in the coach, which carried the mails, etc., for the South. One could not easily forget that trip: it was bump, bump, bump, with an occasional lurch to right or left as the wheels dropped into a rut or went over a root or piece of timber that was thrown down to stop the wheels going too deep. ... I was at a disadvantage through having to hold my baby with one arm.

The journey continued, with the horses often 'kneedeep' in mud.

At last we reached Mr Kennedy's residence, where we were welcomed by one of the kindest families it has ever been my lot to meet. . My husband arranged to meet us there. ... After tea, a good night's rest, and a hearty breakfast the next morning, we started for Jumbunna East, about 19 miles distant. It was a great undertaking, as we had to ride on horseback all the way, and it was my first experience of the kind. We could not go out of a walk, so I was able to sit on. My husband carried the baby on his left arm, with a large shawl tied over his right shoulder, forming a sling or hammock for arm and baby.

About 2 0'clock we reached Mr Blew's place at Whitelaw, and received every kindness from them. After about an hour's rest we had to mount horses again and push on, as the days were short, and we had a long way to go. As we advanced the road got narrower and more difficult, and instead of riding two or three abreast, we had to go in single file. We reached Mr Rainbow's place at Jumbunna East about sunset, very tired and thankful to get to bed that night.

After a stay of a week or ten days, the party continued

We again mounted our horses to proceed to Kongwak, our proper destination. We plunged into a very narrow bridle track, where we could touch the trees on either side and could not see the sky in some places, so dense was the scrub. Our horses had to scramble over logs and through mud knee deep nearly all the way. Occasionally we had to duck our heads to avoid overhanging branches. At last we came to what was supposed to be a clearing on top of a very high hill, from which we could look down on the tops of the trees all round, except the narrow ridge where we came out, and on a ledge some 200 feet below my husband pointed out what appeared to be some galvanized iron on top of a pile of logs, and said, "This is your home." At first I could not speak, and my eyes filled with tears. That one spot of iron, in the midst of a sea of logs and stumps, looked so desolate that my heart failed me for the moment.

However, after scrambling over logs, etc., we managed to get to the cabin, which, on closer inspection, proved to be logs piled one on top of the other in chock and log fashion ... There was a large fireplace, made of wood outside and lined with stones and mud. There were also windows and a door, but it was not easy to get inside as there was a huge stump in the doorway. My husband had brought down some flooring boards on horseback, and had made a table with what was left over after flooring the two rooms, so I settled the baby on the table, and prepared the refreshments my friend had so kindly packed for us.

Mrs Williams goes on to describe how she stopped up the cracks in the walls using strips of tree ferns and covering them with hessian and paper. The two of them made some furniture out of pine boards and blackwood logs. *"We made a sofa, cot, and two easy chairs, which, when covered with cretonne, looked very nice and comfortable"*. She goes on, *"All this kind of work had to be done at night, as there was fencing, clearing, etc., to be done in the daytime."*

Her husband, William, one day went off on a draught horse to collect a pig from a neighbour. *"About noon I could hear in the distance some awful squealing ... By and by he appeared with a good-sized pig in a bag in front of him, struggling and squealing at a great rate".* A little later, some neighbours were invited to come fishing in the river and to share a meal afterwards. After failing to catch any fish, *"we started for home feeling very tired and hungry, to find on our arrival that the pig had been there before us, and had destroyed what he could not eat."*

When provisions were needed, Mrs Williams' husband made a 19-mile trip to the store, leading a pack horse to carry the load. This would leave his wife alone until late at night. A huge goanna (an 'iguana') once frightened her and, trembling, she took a gun and shot it dead. Her husband laughed when he returned, which was no comfort. Earlier, a passing stranger had caused her some alarm. Despite her isolation and her anxieties, this pioneer woman found peace and even exhilaration in the midst of the forbidding forest:

All night the dingoes would set up the most dismal howl that made one's blood run cold, and the roar and screams of the bears would echo through the forest, but when the day broke the singing of the birds and the sweet smell of the shrubs would make one forget the fears of the night before, and thank God for the beauties of nature. Oh! how I used to love the early mornings, when everything awoke to new life; I would just stand and feast on the beauty and glory of it all.

She ends her account in a manner typical of her time:

I have reason to believe I was the first white woman to come to Kongwak, and my second son was the first child born there. While I write he is on the battlefield of France, fighting for his King and Country, with, I trust, the same courage and tenacity his father showed when trying to make a home in the forest of South Gippsland. *

[*I'm happy to report that Gunner Francis Oliver Williams, 59th Battalion, returned safely to Australia after his war service.]

Lady of the Swamp

The disappearance of Miss Margaret Clement from her South Gippsland home in 1952 was a tragedy at many levels. In the unravelling of the several layers of mystery involved, the one thing mostly missing is compassion for Miss Clement herself. I'll try to keep that in mind as I re-tell the story.

Peter Clement struck it lucky during the Walhalla gold rush. He bought shares in the Long Tunnel mine at an early stage and saw his investment increase astronomically. He bought a number of first-class properties, including Prospect Station, at Seaspray, one of Gippsland's most historic estates. Clement married a much younger woman. She bore him six children who grew up in very comfortable circumstances in Sale. In 1907, with proceeds from the father's will, two of the children, Jeannie and Margaret, together with their mother, bought a prime property in South Gippsland, near Buffalo. It covered 1875 acres, much of it excellent grazing land, and included a fourteen-room brick and timber home, 'Tullaree'. The Tarwin River ran through the property. Much of the land was low-lying and prone to flooding. However, a network of drains and levees kept the land from being inundated.

Money was no object. The girls enjoyed a life of luxury, especially after they turned twenty-one and came into their father's inheritance. They attended fashionable balls; they travelled overseas; their future seemed assured. Their two sisters – Flora and Anna – married. The boys went their own way. Jeannie and Margaret remained at Tullaree, just the two of them. Without experience in the ways of the world, the two fell victim to confidence tricksters and poor management, and lost a great part of their wealth. There was no money to keep the property in good order. As the years passed, the drains became choked; the banks collapsed inwards. The house became a ruin, surrounded by a sea of swampland, the level of water rising and falling with the seasons and the weather. The two elderly spinsters would pick their way through the swamp to walk into Buffalo for supplies. They were regarded as eccentrics. And then, in 1950, Jeannie died.

Margaret carried on alone. She vowed never to leave the homestead. 'I am now alone, except for Dingo, my dog,' she told a reporter in 1951, 'but I won't be a bit frightened.' The house was now in ruins. There was no power, sewerage, or piped water. Margaret became a pathetic figure as she made her way to and from the house through the dangerous, snake-infested marshes surrounding the house. Meanwhile, there was a legal shadow over the property. In an earlier will, Margaret had left a share of Tullaree to a nephew, her sister, Anna's son, Clem Carnaghan, but in 1951 she revoked the will, disinheriting him and sold the property to a neighbourhood couple, Stan and Esme Livingstone for £3000. The Livingstones also took over a £12, 500 mortgage on the place. The nephew later contested this action at law, unsuccessfully, on the grounds of Margaret's mental condition at the time.

At Tullaree strange things began to happen. Some men tried to entice Margaret from a car in Tarwin Lower. Later, some men in 'a big black English car' appeared, asking directions to 'the haunted house where the old swamp lady lives'. Anonymous letters posted in New South Wales containing religious messages dwelling on death were sent though the post. Mysterious visitors appeared at the property. Some recalled that many years earlier, a hoard of 5,000 stolen gold sovereigns had been stashed away on the property by a previous owner and only part of the treasure had been retrieved. And then, Margaret's dog, 'Dingo', died, its throat savaged in a peculiar way. 'Wild allegations are being made,' said Senior Detective Bryan Traynor of Warragul CIB.

On the night of 15 May, 1952, Stan Livingstone heard his dogs barking ferociously. The next day, he knocked on Margaret Clement's door. There was no answer. After a delay of several days, Livingstone called the police. A widespread search was undertaken. Over the next two weeks a dozen police and up to twenty local men combed the marshes. Some reports had it that 100 men were involved. Newspaper photographs of the time show men wading through waist-deep water. Some rode horses. Some drove tractors. A motor-boat was used at one stage. Stan Livingstone himself brought in a bulldozer that smashed down the old tracks through the swamp. A blacktracker was brought in from Melbourne. Clem Carnaghan hired a private detective. Over several months, the search extended to the area surrounding Tullaree itself. Nothing was found. A surge of renewed excitement occurred when the skeleton of a female was found in sand dunes on the coast nearby, but it led to nothing. The skeleton was probably that of an aboriginal woman, it was found. Eventually, the search was called off. Two years later, a court decided officially that Margaret Clement was dead.

Theories about her death abounded. The original view that she had wandered into the swamp, fallen or collapsed, and drowned was soon discarded. Margaret knew the waterways too well. And after all, no body was found. But there was one other matter that was of pivotal importance. Margaret never ventured outside the house without her walking stick – and the walking stick was found inside the house after her disappearance. The only conclusion left was that she had been taken by someone or some others, and probably against her will.

Some believed that Carl Carnaghan was involved in his aunt's disappearance, but the main suspicion fell on Stan Livingstone. He was reputed to be a man ready to push his weight around. On one occasion he had punched Clem Carnaghan on the jaw. He was a former Footscray footballer (sixteen games; three goals!) and strongly built. His wife Esme seemed to live in some fear of him. During one interview with the police, she refused to speak, apparently for fear of her husband. It was widely spoken of that she had admitted to friends in the neighbourhood that her husband was involved in Margaret's death. One of these friends even provided the information that Livingstone had brought in two Melbourne thugs to get rid of Margaret. There is no doubt that police regarded Livingstone as their main suspect, but nothing could be proved against him. On the surface, it is not easy to see what would have motivated Livingstone to arrange for the old lady's murder. He had already secured possession of the property and the continued presence of Margaret alongside him would seem of little consequence. Maybe Margaret knew something about those hidden sovereigns!

Stan Livingstone sold Tullaree for £67,500 five years after Margaret died, and moved with Esme to Queensland. He died in 1992, a wealthy man. Esme died in a Morwell Nursing Home the next year. As for Tullaree, it has been restored to its former glory ... and more. It is now one of the show pieces of South Gippsland.

To the outsider, the life of Margaret Clement is one of infinite sadness. The early years of bright promise ended in later years of lonely disappointment. After her death, her privacy, which she treasured so much, was invaded by a mindless public eager for sensation and excitement. In all likelihood she suffered shock and pain in the manner of her passing. She has no memorial stone to commemorate her.

Yet she never gave in to the difficulties which came to her. She maintained a lively and outgoing disposition. She lived in a place which, though broken and tumbledown, was precious to her, and she was there until the end. She will always remain one of Gippsland's special people.